Missions Made Fun for Kids

CREATIVE IDEAS TO INVOLVE Children in Missions

Elizabeth Whitney Crisci

ACCENT PUBLICATIONS
Colorado Springs, Colorado

Accent Publications
4050 Lee Vance View
P.O. Box 36640
Colorado Springs, Colorado 80936

Library of Congress Catalog Card Number 92-71091
ISBN 0-89636-306-6

Third Printing

Contents

96851

Introduction

Missions Made Fun for Kids is a book of ideas. It presents the cause of missions in an exciting, interesting, upbeat way while impressing young minds with the need and responsibility to serve God as witnesses.

The ideas in this book are not meant to be used in any order. Nor are they meant to be used every week. These "fun" ideas might be used as a monthly activity. Different ideas might be tried every week for a month. *Missions Made Fun for Kids* might be used for several weeks leading up to a missionary conference or as a follow-up afterward.

Take a few moments to read through the book. Look for the ideas that will allow you to bring the work of missions and the privilege of serving the Lord as a witness before your class often in ways that speak to them. *Missions Made Fun for Kids* emphasizes both the global outreach of missions and ways for children and youth to see how they can be missionaries right now, where they live. Look for the "Alternatives" at the end of several ideas.

Missions must never be put in the background of our teaching. Our Christian service will become stagnant quickly if it is, and God's work will die. We are stewards of God's truth. The world needs each believer to enjoy the true purpose of missions — introducing others to our Savior, anywhere, anytime.

Suggestions

We are servant/witnesses of the grace of Jesus Christ. The work of a missionary at home or on a foreign field is a divine imperative. Jesus Himself gave these instructions to all of His followers, "As my father hath sent me, even so send I you" (John 20:21). There are no exceptions to our Lord's command.

Decide now that the missionary message will not be side-lined in your classroom. Make it a vital part of the lessons you teach. Even when the lessons seem to have other themes, missions can always become part of the message.

Missions is God's way of telling others that His Son came to earth to live, die, and rise again for their salvation.

If we as teachers in Christian schools, in youth groups, in mid-week clubs, in Vacation Bible Schools, and in Sunday Schools neglect missions, think of the consequences. If we do not instill that heart-felt need to tell others, the current shortage of missionaries will grow to epidemic proportions. We must not allow the young lives we teach today to fall into spiritual complacency and selfishness with the knowledge of Jesus Christ.

Some suggestions for the use of this book are:
1) Make your lesson plans in advance. Decide when to use a missions emphasis.
2) Select ideas from this book that will work with your particular class. Highlight them on the Contents page. Modify them as you need for the ages and abilities of your students.
3) Use the suggestions more than once, but allow time between each use. Don't overuse a good idea.
4) Pray that these ideas will result in a better understanding about missions and that the students will commit their lives and resources for God's work. Pray that many will accept the challenge of a full-time career in missions work.

I challenge you to foster the missions education of your young people. Ask God to enable you to love missions yourself, to teach the joy of taking God's Word to people who have not heard it, and to make missions exciting for kids so that there will not be such a need in the next generation. For if the current trends continue, the churches in the future may not be able to overcome the lack of those willing to march on the forefront of God's battle lines.

You have the privilege and the opportunity to include the message of missions often and interestingly in your classroom. You are God's missionary to your students. Will you keep the cause of Christ at home and abroad before their tender hearts?

"The things that thou hast heard of me among many witnesses, the same commit thou to faithful men, who shall be able to teach others also" (II Timothy 2:2).

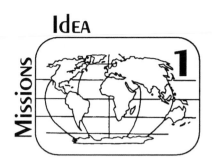

Idea

Missions

1

WHERE iN THE WORld?

PURPOSE:

"Where In The World?" is designed to open up the world as a mission field and to show the students the need for the gospel beyond their city limits.

PREPARATiON:

Before class make copies of the quiz. Distribute one to each student. Be sure the correct answers are handy.

Supplies NEEdEd:

Copy machine or carbon paper, copy paper, pencils, a large globe (preferably) or a world map, whistle.

TiME nEEdEd:

5-6 minutes

WHAT TO do:

Give each student a pencil and a copy of the quiz turned upside down. Explain that at the sound of the whistle, they are to turn their papers over and unscramble the words, which are countries of the world. Allow approximately five (5) minutes to unscramble the countries and then, let different children give the answers.

Those who answer correctly can approach the globe and find where the country is located. Ask the students to think about the continent on which each country is located. Mention one of the missionaries that your church helps to support and who serves in that area. (Change some of the scrambled countries, if necessary, to include your church's missions ministry.) Ask students what kind of people live in these countries. Help them see that the language, ethnic backgrounds, or customs do not matter. They are people just like them who need to hear about Jesus.

Quiz:

WHERE IN THE WORLD?

1. X E M I O C	6. R E T N A I N G A
2. ZMAAATNI	7. I Y T L A
3. Z I L R A B	8. T A A P K S I N
4. A L O P D N	9. K Y E A N
5. DOCMMUR	10. WEN NEIAUG

Answers:

1. Mexico (North America) 6. Argentina (South America)
2. Tasmania (Australia)   7. Italy (Europe)
3. Brazil (South America)   8. Pakistan (Asia)
4. Poland (Europe)   9. Kenya (Africa)
5. McMurdo (Antarctica)   10. New Guinea (Asia)

Projected Results:

The students will gain a broader view of the world and of places where the gospel is needed. They will see the globe (the world) in a practical sense, get an idea where their own church missionaries are serving, and become aware of the fact that even the "civilized" world needs the gospel.

Alternative:

Change the quiz locations to places within your state or streets and areas within your city. Provide a state or city map for students to find the locales. This will help students to realize that God expects us to be "missionaries" in our own areas, too. We do not have to go to a far away or foreign place. Talk about the people who live in these places and why they need Jesus. Discuss what differences there might be in witnessing to these people versus those who live farther away.

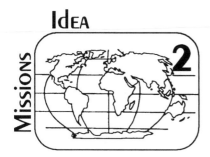

Idea

Missions **2**

LETTER TIME

PURPOSE:

> To acquaint the students with one missionary that the church has an interest in both by financial support and prayer.

PREPARATION:

> Get the name and address of one of your church-supported missionaries.

Supplies Needed:

> Light weight paper, small sheet for each student, pens, large envelope, postage money.

Time Needed:

> Approximately 6-8 minutes.

What to do:

> Explain to the students that they will each write a short letter to a very special person: one of our missionaries. Have a picture displayed on an easel at the front of the classroom. Include an address and a map showing the location geographically. Give a little information about the missionary and list several things about themselves the children might want to write about in their letters.
>
> Some suggestions might be:
> - their age
> - grade in school
> - their hobby
> - favorite sport
> - when they accepted Christ as Savior
> - details of their family or pets

They might want to ask questions like: "What do you eat in your country?" or, "What is the climate like?"

Hand out the paper and pens. Give them several minutes to write their short letter, including their name and address. Meanwhile you, as the teacher, should have a letter to the missionary ready to include with theirs. Explain why you are writing and that you will be praying for that family or missionary. Let a student who prints clearly address the envelope, and have another student put the letters in the envelope. Ask one or more students to go to the Post Office with you during the week, if possible. Show genuine enthusiasm as a teacher and it will rub off on the students!

Projected Results:

The students will be excited about mailing their letters. They will feel personally involved with that missionary and will anxiously await an answer. Warn them, however, that the missionaries are busy people, and it may take some time to get an answer back from their mission field. But take time when the answer does arrive to read it, discuss it, and post it on the bulletin board.

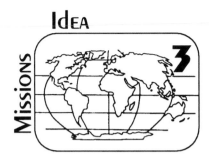

IdEA

Missions

3

Verse-A-Gram

Purpose:

To keep the Word of God and its missionary challenges before the children as often as possible. It is the Word that brings commitment to missions.

Preparation:

Prepare a large cardboard with the Bible verse: "PRAY YE THEREFORE THE LORD OF THE HARVEST, THAT HE WILL SEND FORTH LABOURERS INTO HIS HARVEST" (Matthew 9:38). Cut it up so that each word is on a separate piece.

Supplies Needed:

Cardboard or posterboard (at least 12 x 18 inches), wide felt-tip marker, scissors, table for displaying the verse.

Time Needed:

5-10 minutes

What to do:

Place the Bible verse, in its correct order, on the table before the students. Have them stand around the table. Read the verse to the class; ask the class to read it with you; ask them to read it without you. Ask one student to read it alone, aloud. Then pick up all the cards, mix them up, and place them on the table again in whatever order they come from the pile. Ask the students to straighten it out.

Read the verse as a class again. Then ask the last

reader to mix the cards up again and put them back on the table in whatever order they come. Ask each member of the class to pick up a piece and to stand in the order of the verse. Say it aloud together again. After repeating this procedure two or three times, hide the words and see if everyone can say the verse. Close with prayer that the Lord will indeed send workers into His harvest, even some from this very class!

The students will learn, in word and in deed, Matthew 9:38. As you prepare, "PRAY YE THEREFORE THE LORD OF THE HARVEST, THAT HE WILL SEND FORTH LABOURERS INTO HIS HARVEST." And that they might come from your students! Talk about what the verse means.

Projected Results:

A Bible verse will be hidden in the hearts of the students. They will have fun as they learn the verse, and they will realize that God speaks to them personally in His Word, too.

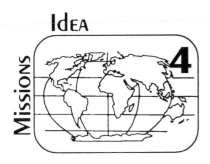

VillAqE LifE

PURPOSE:

To acquaint students with the way missionaries live, as well as the people they serve: including their homes, their food, their dress.

PREPARATION:

Bring pictures into class showing villages, cities, homes, clothing, and food if possible. If you do the field of one of your church's missionaries, this will mean either a letter to the field to secure the necessary information and obtain photographs, or inquire while the missionary is in the area on home furlough. Or, you may want to select a different area or mission field to study to help students learn about other places. Make a sample house and a sample figure of a local person.

Supplies NEEdEd:

Collect sticks, grasses, artificial trees, and plants. Ask the students and other church members to bring in items that would help in the building of the place you have chosen. Also, have a supply of cardboard, scraps of cloth, pins, needles and thread, etc. A large piece of plywood or masonite (about three feet square) would be best for the bottom of the village. Have glue, heavy shears, scissors, paints, and clay available. Clothespins make good foundations for villagers.

TimE NEEdEd:

7-15 minutes a week for a month

What to do:

The week before the project is to begin, explain it to the class, and bring in the photographs and even a sample or two of homes/huts or people. Ask for help in the collection of needed supplies. **The first week:** Make the area including grasses, trees, flowers, etc. **The second week:** Make the houses. **The third week:** Make some people with clothing distinctive to the area. **The fourth week:** Make some food, and put the village/city/town together.

It would be an excellent idea to display the finished product in the church for everyone to appreciate what the children have done, and to learn about the special place where one of your church's missionaries is serving.

When you finish, spend some time praying for the people and missionaries in the place you have built.

Projected Results:

The class will be knit together in a project for the Lord. They will learn to work side by side. They will learn the difficulties a missionary faces in a different society. They will learn how other people live. They will be burdened for the work of missions and they will probably get excited about God's work overseas. And best of all, pray that some will be called by God as they reach adulthood, and that they will answer His call.

Alternative:

Have students do the same thing for a place or area within your state. Emphasize that there are people who need to hear about Jesus in small towns close to them as well as in places overseas. You could build a relief map of the state, look up distinctives that make your state unique, show homes and people who may be different from your immediate area. If most of your students live in an urban environment, look at the farm or rural areas. If your students live in the suburbs, look at inner-city life.

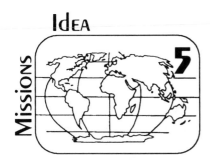

Idea

Missions

5

Picture This Land

Purpose:

"PICTURE THIS LAND" is planned to show the students an area of the world that is foreign to them. It should reveal houses, home life, clothing, food, characteristics, festivals, religions, and customs. Such information, presented interestingly, will generate a wider world view and produce a praying concern for missions.

Preparation:

Find old *National Geographic* magazines. Match one with a good pictorial article with a missionary the church supports. From another country featured in a *Geographic,* make a small (maybe 9" x 12" inch) sample. Get a prayer card and a prayer letter of the missionary to be featured. Highlight the most important parts of the prayer letter to shorten the reading time.

Supplies Needed:

Old *National Geographics*, one large piece of posterboard, felt markers, rubber cement (or paste), scissors, a table to work on, picture of the missionary (prayer card), a recent prayer letter, and a highlighter pen.

Time Needed:

10 minutes at the most (Don't prolong it.)

What to do:

Display the small sample of the poster. Show the missionary's picture and ask a student to read the highlighted part of a prayer letter. Then put the supplies on the table, carefully remove the appropriate pages from the magazine, and have the children make an attractive collage of the missionary's field of service. They should read the captions (silently), so they can neatly print an explanation.

Be sure they include the homes, the foods, the dress, the customs, the religions, and any other pertinent facts they can discover. Help those who might sit back and let the others take over by handing them several pictures and getting them started in the process.

Projected Results:

Informed students whose interest in another part of the world has been piqued will know where their missionary is serving. Praying students will know better how to pray for their missionary. Plus, some students may see the Lord leading them into that very area of the world to serve.

Alternative:

You can do the same project with a map of your state or nation. Pick a place far enough away that the majority of your students will not have been there. Look at the houses, home life, clothing, food, characteristics, festivals, religions, and customs. Inner-city areas, Indian reservations, or Amish areas are especially interesting. When students see that these people are just like them for the most part, they will begin to realize that everyone needs to know about Jesus, not just people whose lives are completely different.

National Geographic articles on places within your country can be used just as well as articles on foreign locations. Your church may have missionaries to the Indians, to the inner-city, to various groups whom you can use for this project. If not, encourage students to look for needs that they might be able to fulfill as missionaries to that region.

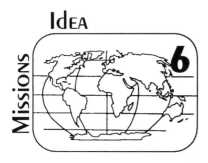

IdEA

Missions

6

Adoption Agency

PurposE:

To make the children aware of missionary children, their problems, their blessings, and their needs.

PreparatioN:

Select several missionary families the church helps support. Each should have a child about the same age as those in the class. Find out the addresses, the birthdays, and procure pictures. Get all the supplies before class begins.

Supplies NeedEd:

Picture and information about "missionary kids," felt-tip pens calligraphy pens, regular pens, heavy duty paper (8" x 10"—one per child), plus two with "Certificate of Adoption" at the top, ruler, two frames, mailing necessities.

TimE NeedEd:

6-7 minutes plus continuing follow-up

WhaT to do:

Explain to the students that you would like them to "adopt" a missionary kid to be their special friend. Show the pictures, explain the situation, country, family information, dangers, schooling, health, where the MKs were born, hobbies, etc. Ask for a vote as to which child the class would like to adopt as their own.

Then, give each student paper that has been printed with words similar to these:

CERTIFICATE OF ADOPTION

The 199____ Sunday School Class of

_____ Church

hereby adopts:

_____

to be their very own MK.

We, the class members, promise to pray for you, write to you, remember your birthday, and keep you as our special friend for one whole year.

Signed (by the class members):

_____	_____
_____	_____
_____	_____
_____	_____

Have each student sign each one of the Certificates of Adoption. Choose the neatest one to frame and mail to the missionary child. The next best one hang up on the bulletin board. The others can be taken home and used to remind the students to pray for their adopted friend and long-distance class member.

Projected Results:

This project should generate a prayer interest never before seen among your young people, perhaps even a desire to go to the field where this child lives. There will be a genuine interest in this child when the family comes home on furlough.

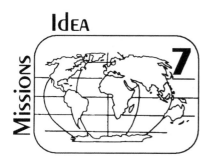

Idea

Missions

7

Mission Restaurant

Purpose:

To allow the students to "taste" a mission field; to spend extra time with the students and sense their needs.

Preparation:

Select a country where one of your church-supported missionaries serves. It might be one that the class has already selected as its own missionary. **Check** with the missionary or an encyclopedia and find out their foods. **Ask** someone in the church to be the cook for a MISSION RESTAURANT occasion you are planning. **Set** a date and place for the meal. **Select** an INVITATION COMMITTEE to start working two weeks in advance. Be sure to **invite** the pastor and/or other church staff members. Parents or siblings could be invited, as well.

Supplies Needed:

Invitations, special foods, pencils, copied menus, short film, slides, or speaker.

Time Needed:

About 1-1/2 hours outside of class time, plus planning and preparation

What to do:

Announce the MISSION RESTAURANT two or three weeks in advance. Ask two students to make and send out or give the invitations two weeks in advance. Mail one to every absentee and take reservations. You will need two or more to decorate, two to help the volunteer cook, and at least three students to help clean up.

Include not only the foreign dish (which some may not like) but also pizza, hamburgers, or some other familiar dish. For the program, keep it brief, with a couple of table games (from the country, if possible) and a brief message via film, slides, or speaker.

Sample Invitation:

YOU ARE INVITED
TO OUR MISSION RESTAURANT

at

_____

Date: _____ Time: _____

R.S.V.P. To:_____

Phone #:_____

One suggested game might include:

Scrambled Menu

Figure out what you are eating.
Unscramble the words below to see tonight's dinner.

1) H C C I N K E (chicken)   2) C E I R   (rice)

3) R D B A E   (bread)   4) N A A A N B   (banana)

5) K M L I   (milk)   6) G P I   (pig)

7) I F H S   (fish)   8) E C A K   (cake)

Be sure to close with prayer for the missionaries who are being remembered in MISSION RESTAURANT.

Projected Results:

A deeper interest in the mission field, perhaps a better understanding that one could adjust to different kinds of food if God should call them to the mission field, and a deeper appreciation for those who have gone and must eat foods that are "different" all the time.

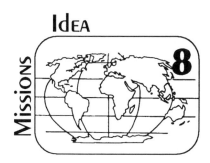

IdEA

Missions

8

Tape-Away

PURPOSE:

> To get to know a missionary, to know his/her needs, and to learn to pray for those needs.

PREPARATION:

> Discover a missionary that the students should get to know more closely. Get the address and learn the family situation and the location.

Supplies Needed:

> Tape recorder, blank tape, mailing envelope, the missionary's address and stamps.

Time Needed:

> 5-6 minutes in class, plus the preparation time and lesson time

What to do:

> Show the class a picture (if possible) and describe the missionaries to be talked to, the country in which they serve, the marital status, the children, the type of ministry (teaching, medical, agriculture, church planting, aviation, translation, house parents, etc.).
>
> Then tell the students they are going to talk to the missionaries on a tape that they will mail to them. Explain that it is important for everyone to be very quiet during the taping.
>
> Begin the tape with an introduction by the teacher. Add a Bible verse said in unison. (You may want soft

background music for this.) Or sing a special song together.

Then each child should tell:
    his/her name,
    grade in school,
    favorite sport or hobby,
    a favorite food or color,
    a favorite animal or the name of a pet,
    favorite subject in school,
    the names of sisters and brothers.

After each one reports, begin the lesson and keep the tape recorder going. Close the class session in prayer with each student praying specifically for the missionaries. The missionaries will get in on the lesson, be touched by the prayers for them that they can hear, and the students will probably behave better because they are being "heard" in a faraway country!

Projected Results:

The students will share their lives with real missionaries along with the excitement and hope for an answer from somewhere far away. A well-disciplined class should occur because of the recording of the class lesson. The answer from the mission family chosen will help students realize missionaries are real people with real families just like theirs.

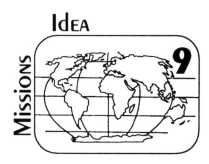

Idea

Missions 9

FOREIGN EXAM

PURPOSE:

To show the difficulties and the blessings of the foreign mission field and to reveal the possibilities of going overseas for the Lord.

PREPARATION:

Copy the FOREIGN EXAM (one per student) and be sure there are pencils and work space available.

SUPPLIES NEEDED:

Copied papers, answers, pencils, and table.

TIME NEEDED:

5 minutes

WHAT TO DO:

Explain that, "Tests don't have to be scary; they can be fun, especially when there will be no grade given." Pass out the FOREIGN EXAM and at the count of three, let them begin.

When everyone has finished, take time to go over the answers and ask for discussion about any of the points that might be puzzling. Suggest they take their FOREIGN EXAM home and let their families take the exam, too. You may want to give each child a blank test to take home.

FOREIGN EXAM

1) Write hello in a foreign language. _____

2) What is your favorite foreign country? _____

   Why?_____

3) Name two countries where you know missionaries

   serving Jesus._____

4) Have you ever thought about being a missionary?

   Yes_____No_____

   Where?_____

   Why?_____

5) What does a missionary do to reach people for

   Jesus? _____

   _____

6) What do you think is the hardest part of being a

   foreign missionary? _____

   _____

7) What is the best part of being a foreign missionary?

   _____

8) What dangers do missionaries face?_____

   _____

9) What do most missionaries do on the foreign field?

   _____

10) What abilities do I have that God might be able to

    use as a missionary?_____

11) How do you think God calls a missionary?_____

_____

12) What can I do now to be ready if God calls me, when I am older, to be a full-time missionary?_____

_____

13) Does God expect you to be a missionary now?____

14) How can you be a missionary right now, right where you live, and where you go to school? Give some examples. _____

_____

_____

15) I want to tell others about Jesus and I will tell at least one person this week about Him. Yes_____ No____

Projected Results:

The students will think about the mission field and their responsibilities to be witnesses for Jesus now, be better able to pray for missionaries, and consider the mission field as an option in career planning.

Alternative:

Take out the word foreign and encourage children to think of one place in their country and one place in a foreign country when they answer the questions.

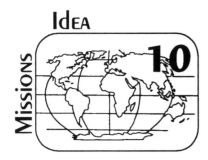

IDEA

Missions

10

POSTER ART

PURPOSE:

To let the students share with the entire church body their interest in missions and to increase their own awareness of what God wants of His church.

PREPARATION:

Find the needed supplies before class. Check with the Pastor and/or your missions committee to see what the current needs are in the area of missions (not just money).

Supplies Needed:

Brightly colored posterboard (1/2 sheet per student), or one big sheet for two to work on together, assorted felt pens, scissors, rubber cement, prayer cards, maps, pictures from the mission field, stencils, old magazines, Bibles.

Time Needed:

8-15 minutes for at least two successive weeks

What to do:

Explain the need to interest the entire church in missions. Their posters, hung in the foyer, will be a good way to make others aware of the need for missions education and the needs of missionaries. Place notices in the church bulletin: "Watch for posters." Or, "The posters are coming — and so is our Missions Conference!"

Explain the needs which have been shared by the

pastor or missions committee and let students take different themes and make posters that will "speak to people." (You may want to ask the pastor or missions committee chairman to come and present the needs themselves.)

Posters can be done with felt pens, hand-drawn pictures, paint, glitter, cut out letters, cut-outs from magazines, stencils, or whatever the student feels would touch hearts and best communicate their message. Bible verses can be printed on the posters. For instance: Matthew 28:19; Mark 16:15; Acts 1:8.

In the first class period, help students plan their poster on scrap paper and get approval to begin. The second week, they should begin their project. Some students or classes may need a third week in order to complete the posters. Give sufficient time so that students can do a good job.

Be sure to get the posters hung in the foyer for them, their parents, and the entire church body to see and respond to for a week.

Projected Results:

The message that the students are trying to convey will reach their hearts and the hearts of others as they work on their posters. They will know that they are helping the whole church become more aware of missions. Make it a point to intercede in prayer for them daily that they will be ready to be missionaries: by praying, by giving, by going.

While you are working with the children on these posters, as well as on other Idea presentations, continue to remind them that missionaries are not all in foreign countries, where people dress and live differently, but that where we live now is a mission field, too. So at school, on the playground, with friends, etc., we can be—and should be—missionaries!

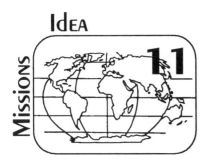

Idea

11

Overseas Relay

Purpose:

To have fun, a break from the seriousness of a lesson, and to get acquainted with ministry opportunities for the Lord.

Preparation:

Prepare on open space for a relay race. Cut out two small pictures of Bibles or draw them, (about six inches in diameter) and glue them on two paper plates.

Supplies Needed:

Chalk, chalkboard, two (2) small pictures of Bibles, two (2) paper plates, two (2) world maps, glue, large space for a relay race. Alternative: State or city map.

Time Needed:

Approximately 6-7 minutes

What to do:

Divide the class into two teams. The fastest and easiest way is to let them number off: one, two, one, two, etc.

The students line up behind a chosen captain. Hand each leader a paper plate with the Bible drawn on it. Mark off a beginning and an ending line with the chalk. Place two chairs at the finish line, and on each chair, place a world map or your state or city map to emphasize that missions does not refer only to a foreign country.

The object of the relay is to get the Bible to the world (or your community) as quickly as possible.

At the signal, the first runner heads for the finish with his BIBLE paper plate. When he reaches the globe or map, he finds a country, places his finger on it, says the name of the country, and then says:
"GO YE INTO ALL THE WORLD AND PREACH THE
GOSPEL TO EVERY CREATURE."
Mark 16:15

He then races back to the next runner in line and hands him the plate. Each runner does the same thing, but says the name of a different country. The team that finishes first is the winner.

Try it a second time, but this time let the teams walk backward. Explain: "Some people are hindered in bringing the gospel to the world because of the lack of money, the lack of prayers, the lack of people. Some people who should be missionaries, stay home because they love this world and its attractions. *All of us* should be missionaries *right now, right where we are,* but we don't realize it."

Congratulate the winning team and emphasize that getting the message out to the world far away or our world right where we live, is more than a game. We all must get personally involved.

Projected Results:

A relaxing time between serious study, a fun interlude which makes this game's message memorable, and a lasting message of missions. Help the children to understand that when God's Word says, "Go into all the world and preach the gospel to every creature" that every creature means those all around us, too.

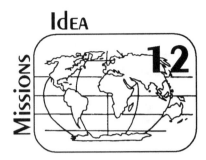

IdEA

Missions

12

INSECT RebElliON

PurposE:

To show the students that the mission field is not glamorous. God helps missionaries through difficulties, but it is hard to be in an unknown territory serving the Lord.

PREPARATioN:

Copy the quiz: one per student.

SuppliEs NEEdEd:

Puzzle pages, pencils, answers

TimE NEEdEd:

4-5 minutes

WHAT TO do:

Give each student a copy of the quiz, placed upside-down. At the count of three, ask them to turn the sheets right-side up and begin. The first one finished can begin the answers, but let others also give their answers.

INSECT REBELLION

1) Unscramble the letters:

    a) IERDSP   b) CCCOOKRAH

    c) LNGYFI NAT   d) TSULOC

2) Unscramble the letters:

   a) KSENA   b) GTIER

   c) YNAHE   d) ILON

3) Unscramble the words and put them in the right order:
   REFUGE   AND   EVER-PRESENT   GOD
   TROUBLE   IS   IN   HELP   OUR
   STRENGTH   AN   PSALM 46:1

4) Finish the answer: I could go into the jungle for Jesus if:

   _____

   _____

5) Finish the answer: Missionaries should go to the mission field because...

   _____

   _____

6) Choose the best answer: Missionaries can face poisonous snakes and insects because:
   a) they are braver than I am.
   b) they close their eyes to insects.
   c) they trust the Lord to help them.
   d) they select safe places.

ANSWERS:
1) spider, cockroach, flying ant, locust
2) snake, tiger, hyena, lion
3) God is our refuge and strength, an ever-present help in trouble. Psalm 46:1
4) and 5) personal opinion
6) c

Projected Results:

Students will enjoy the quiz because it isn't for a grade. It will help them think about how to face frightening experiences here or abroad, and see that God can help them in any "scary" situation.

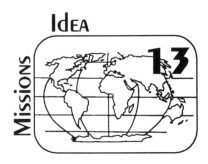

IdEA

Missions

13

Questions for Kids

Purpose:

To let the students ask any question they wish, without fear, and let their peers answer those questions, with a teacher-advisor helping only when necessary.

Preparation:

Think of questions that a young person might ask about the mission field, home or abroad, or use the ones listed below. Write them down.

Supplies Needed:

Scrap paper, pencils, globe or maps of the world, your state, your city.

Time Needed:

4-5 minutes

What to do:

Announce the project to the class as:
"QUESTIONS FOR KIDS"
Begin by saying, "We are going to think about Missions today. I'm going to try to keep quiet. You will ask the questions and you will answer them. But each question must be related to the work of missions. This means questions about being missionaries now, as well as waiting until you are through school, or college, or training school. Each answer should be honest and Christ-like."

Read your list of questions given below as examples, but tell the students that they must think up their own.

Keep your own record of their questions and answers so that you can address any concerns or misinformation later.

Divide the class into two groups, with a captain for each. The captain is to see that each team member gets an opportunity to ask questions and answer others, if desired.

Group 1 will ask questions for two minutes. Group 2 will answer. Then switch for the last two minutes.

Suggested sample questions:
1) How would you define a missionary?
2) Can someone like me be a missionary now, or do I have to wait until I have finished college, seminary, or Bible school?
3) How can someone like me be a missionary? (Give a specific example.)
4) Can I be a missionary by living like a person who loves Jesus?
5) Can I expect some kids to make fun of me when I witness about Jesus Christ?
6) How do you think natives of a foreign land might treat missionaries who are foreigners to them?

Projected Results:

Becoming "missions conscious" ought to result. Also, the teacher will get insights into the students' personal opinions and may be able to correct wrong ideas in future lessons.

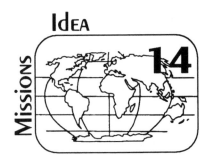

14

World Conflict

Purpose:

To have fun with a missions theme.

Preparation:

Find an open area to play the game. Mark out three circles with chalk equidistant from the center of a large play area.

Supplies Needed:

A ball with the rough outline of the world drawn on it with felt markers, chalk, large open space.

Time Needed:

10 minutes

What to do:

Divide the class into at least three teams: HINDUS, MUSLIMS, BUDDHISTS, and/or CHRISTIANS.

Each team stands in a separate circle at the edge of the play area. The leader places the globe-ball in the center dot and from the side line calls out two teams.
"HINDUS and MUSLIMS!"

These two teams race toward the globe-ball and attempt to carry it back to their own circle.

If the ball carrier is tagged between the shoulder and the elbow, the tagger gets 25 points for his/her team and the globe-ball which they then try to get back to their circle. But if the globe-ball carrier gets back to his/her own circle limits without getting tagged, that team gets 50 points. After 30 seconds, if none of the teams get points, the globe-ball is placed back on the center dot and everyone returns to his/her own circle.

The leader calls out two teams again. If a team is alert, they can get the globe-ball before the others and get back to their own circle. The other team can try to knock the ball out of their opponents' hands, and/or tag the carrier, but there is to be no tripping, shoving, hitting, or tackling. The team members can walk (not run) as fast as they can.

The leader is the sole judge and the teams must abide by the leader's decision. If the teacher feels it would be better, appoint one dependable student to help with the judging.

After the allotted time, declare the winning team with the highest score. Talk about what happened when the other team was wandering in and around the players. Was it harder to accomplish your goal?

Quote John 14:6: "JESUS SAITH UNTO HIM, I AM THE WAY, THE TRUTH AND THE LIFE: NO MAN COMETH UNTO THE FATHER BUT BY ME." Add that any people or religion without the knowledge of Jesus as God's Son and Saviour is a false religion. We must reach them with the gospel.

Projected Results:

Spend a short amount of time explaining some world religions which are false religions because they do not believe or teach that Jesus is the only Way to be saved.

This should make the children alert to the idea that is so prevalent in our society—that, "You're OK just as long as you believe in some religion."

Idea

15 Soccer Around the Globe

Missions

Purpose:

To help the students have a fun time and to continue to stress the fact that there are people around the world and their neighborhood for whom Christ died and who need to hear about Him.

Preparation:

Find a floor space big enough for a circle of chairs to accommodate the entire class.

Supplies Needed:

Chairs, chalkboard and chalk, soccer ball, large open space

Time Needed:

Approximately 8-10 minutes

What to do:

Have the students sit in the circle.

The leader should be "IT" and stand in the center of the circle. It is the leader's job to throw the soccer ball to someone in the circle. That person must then pass the ball (no throwing) to the player on the right, who passes it to the next one to the right, etc. until the leader shouts:

"SOCCER AROUND THE GLOBE,
ONE, TWO, THREE, FOUR, FIVE."

The student with the ball at that time must call out the name of a country before the count of five. If that player doesn't call out a country in the time limit, or calls one that has already been used, he/she becomes a third of a mango. When a student becomes a whole mango, he/she must drop out. Most likely the game will not go on that long. No country can be called out twice, so they must constantly be thinking of new countries. The leader should keep the pace fast and keep the ball moving.

At the close, simply state, "The people in all those countries you have named need to know about Jesus. Let's pray regularly that God will help us to get the message to them. (Because there may be too much excitement at that moment to pause for prayer, be sure to pray for sending the gospel around the world at the end of the class period.)

Projected Results:

Children have a good time, a message of missions gets across, and, an awareness of the need for missions is aroused.

Alternative:

Include the counties or cities in your state or the states/provinces/districts in your country as places that students can call out.

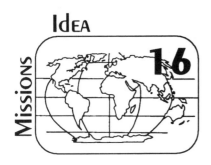

PiN ThE BiblE

PURPOSE:

To get a better idea of the mission fields of the world and develop a concern for them in an interesting way!

PREPARATION:

Place a map of the world on an easel or bulletin board at a height reachable by the students. Make small (one half by one inch (1/2 x 1") cardboard Bibles. Clear a space for the students to play.

Supplies Needed:

Cardboard to make Bibles and to back the map, black felt-tip markers, straight pins, easel, map of the world.

Time Needed:

About 5-10 minutes

What to do:

Ask the students to line up across the room from the easel. Blindfold one student at a time and hand him/her a small cardboard Bible with a pin stuck through it.

Explain that the purpose is to pin the Bible at a place where there is a need to share Christ. The open ocean will not work, but any country or island will be all right (including North America and any state within the United States).

The student then lifts the blindfold off and must identify the place where the Bible is pinned. If the Bible lands far from any land, either let the student select the nearest country, try again, or pass his turn to the next person.

After each student has had an opportunity to "PIN THE BIBLE," pause for prayer. Explain that each one should pray for the country on which she/he "PINNED THE BIBLE." The teacher will begin the prayer, and in the middle of the prayer, pause for a few seconds, to let each student pray either silently or aloud. Conclude the prayer with praise for the concern of the class for missions and the souls of other people.

Projected Results:

A relaxed and interesting way to "see the world" and to get a burden for missions everywhere in it; to pray for the many mission fields suggested by the Bibles pinned on the world map.

Alternative:

Use a map of your state or country instead of the world.

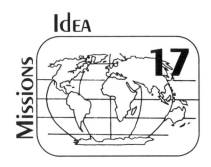

Idea

17

Jungle Adventure

Purpose:

To let the students experience a little bit of primitive living to arouse their curiosity and, hopefully, their desire to serve the Lord. To help them know that the "hardships" aren't as bad as they may imagine and if that is where God has called them, He will also make them content/happy in that place.

Preparation:

Think through a situation and be prepared to help the students put on a skit.

Supplies Needed:

3 x 5 cards, posterboard, pens, actors (students), stage area (can be just the front of the classroom).

Time Needed:

8-10 minutes

What to do:

Explain that the students are to make up a skit. Half the students are to be natives in a jungle village that has never before heard the gospel. The other half of the students are to be a missionary team. The cards and posterboard are to be used to print props: tree, grass hut, cook stove, Bible, chicken or whatever. The students can think ahead and plan who they want to be (like chief, medicine man, mother, child, etc. And the others: missionaries, missionaries' children, guide, interpreter, etc.). Allow them only two minutes for preparation. Have the missionary team arrive and carry on a conversation like:

"Hello."

"Hello."

"I've come to tell you about God."

"About who?"

Give a few suggestions, but let them develop their own conversation. Perhaps the native family could invite them to eat; the medicine man might try to throw them out of the village; the chief might be the first to believe. At the end of the eight minutes, tell them to conclude. Then, the class can close that part of the session with prayer for a missionary family the church is concerned about and for the people with whom they work.

Projected Results:

A keen interest will be aroused in the work of the Lord in faraway places. Most likely, the next missionary speaker will be listened to more attentively because the students will feel like they have experienced a little bit of village living!

Alternative:

Let half of the students be the people on the next street over from where they live. The other half will be a missions team from your church. Prepare the same props for the neighborhood, then have the students develop the skit for that situation. This will help the students realize that they need to talk to those who live closest to them about Jesus, too, and give them a practical idea of how to do it.

IdEA

18

Missions

ModERN EpistLEs

Purpose:

"MODERN EPISTLES" is an attempt to write the way of salvation through Jesus Christ for a faraway country or for anyone nearby who has not heard the gospel.

Preparation:

Select a country where there is a need to hear the gospel. Look it up in an encyclopedia. Also, name a school or schools the children attend, where friends need to hear the gospel.

Supplies Needed:

Paper and pencils

Time Needed:

5-10 minutes

What to do:

Announce the country, and/or the schools; reveal the need for the gospel, and ask the students how they could tell the young people who live there about Jesus.

Ask them to write a letter to a person their own age and explain what they can about Jesus. Share with them that Paul wrote letters (epistles) to places where he had preached, or places that he would like to go to preach and he told them how to know Jesus and how to live for Him.

They might want to share some of Paul's words, like: Romans 3:23: "FOR ALL HAVE SINNED, AND COME

SHORT OF THE GLORY OF GOD."

Romans 6:23: "FOR THE WAGES OF SIN IS DEATH; BUT THE GIFT OF GOD IS ETERNAL LIFE THROUGH JESUS CHRIST OUR LORD."

When they finish their "MODERN EPISTLES," ask them to read them aloud to the class.

Place the finished projects on the bulletin board and encourage the students to share similar "MODERN EPISTLES" at home, by talking to friends or neighbors or writing to people far away, such as distant cousins or pen pals.

Then pray for the results of their "MODERN EPISTLES" as they send them out to people who need Jesus.

Projected Results:

The students will get a clearer picture of salvation for themselves, and they will realize that there are people who don't know how to be saved. They will be better able to share their faith.

Alternative:

Alternatives are built into the directions for this Missions Idea. Help students understand and enjoy the idea of a writing missionary witness as well as a verbal one.

Idea

Missions

19

Ask the Missionary

PURPOSE:

> To let the students become acquainted with a missionary, to see that he/she is human, to learn about the mission field, and to be challenged to serve as a missionary by going, by giving, by praying.

PREPARATION:

> Select a time when a missionary will be at church and request that the he/she come to the class to share with the students. One week before the missionary comes to class, have the students write out two questions they would like to ask a "real, live" missionary. Collect those questions and save them for the following week.

Supplies Needed:

> Small papers, pencils

Time Needed:

> 10 minutes at most

What to do:

> Place the pre-written questions of the students on the table in front of the class. When the missionary arrives, introduce him/her to the class. Ask the visitor to briefly (60 seconds) tell something about himself/herself, and the field where he/she is working. Pre-select two students to come to the front of the class as questioners. Let one read a question from a classmate; then let the other read a question. Alternate between the two readers.

Caution the missionary ahead of time to keep his answers as simple as possible. Give the missionary time to answer, but if the answer gets too complicated, interrupt politely, and say, "We must go on to the next question." (Some adults are not used to working with children and they speak above their heads.)

Try to get through every question that the students wrote out the previous week. At the end of the time, have prayer for the missionary and his/her work.

Projected Results:

A better understanding and a keener interest in the work of missions. The students will want to pray for that particular missionary's work and needs. They will also see that missionaries are just like their friends' fathers and mothers. They will be able to develop a personal interest in other missionaries who come to your church and see them as people they can talk to as well.

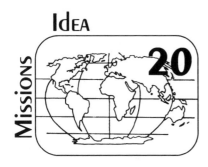

"But I'm Scared"

Purpose:

To show that it is all right to be scared and that God can make difficult things possible.

Preparation:

Prepare a paper, one per student, that says at the top: "BUT I'M SCARED." Think of things that could frighten missionaries and things that could frighten the kids when they try to witness to peers.

Supplies Needed:

Paper, pencils, copier (or pen for hand-printing the phrase "BUT I'M SCARED" onto the papers).

Time Needed:

6-7 minutes

What to do:

Discuss the need for more missionaries in your neighborhood and around the world. Explain that it is not an easy life:

Some go through hard times.
Some die on the mission field.
Some get terrible diseases.
Some are beaten and killed.

Suggest one or two things that would scare people on the mission field: like a new language, being far from friends and family, or snakes and spiders.

Give each student a paper and a pencil. Tell them to

number vertically on their papers, from one to ten (1-10) on the left side. At the count of three, they are to list in one column ten things they think would be scary on the mission field. In a second column, they are to list scary things they feel when they witness to someone at school.

The first one finished is the first one to read his/her list. Take time afterward to show how God can help in each of the difficulties and that God will never put us in a position that does not have a solution.

Close with Hebrews 13:5, "FOR HE HATH SAID, I WILL NEVER LEAVE THEE, NOR FORSAKE THEE" and Philippians 4:13, "I CAN DO ALL THINGS THROUGH CHRIST WHICH STRENGTHENETH ME".

Projected Results:

A certainty of God's presence here or abroad, a realization that it is all right to voice fears of difficulties, and an understanding of how God protects and gives wisdom to those who are serving Him.

IdEA

Missions

21

Jungle Memorandum

Purpose:

To let the students realize that living on the mission field is not too difficult for God's child, that it can be rather normal, even fun. Students will see similarities and differences.

Preparation:

Make enough copies of the list included for each child to have one.

Supplies Needed:

Pencils and the copied list

Time Needed:

8-10 minutes

What to do:

Give each child a list turned upside-down. At the whistle, tell the students to check the column: "like here," "not like here," "easy," and "difficult" after each of the 20 questions. When they are finished, ask one child to read his/her answers to number one, and ask how many agree. Discuss it for a few seconds and do the same with two and all the others. You may want to specify a particular field or area for the students to consider.

THE MISSION FIELD IS:

	LIKE HERE	NOT LIKE HERE	EASY	DIFFICULT
1) Watch TV	___	___	___	___
2) Listen to radio	___	___	___	___
3) Daily shower	___	___	___	___
4) Live at boarding school	___	___	___	___
5) Hot water	___	___	___	___
6) Carry water from stream	___	___	___	___
7) Electricity	___	___	___	___
8) Kerosene lamps	___	___	___	___
9) Pizza store	___	___	___	___
10) Outdoor market	___	___	___	___
11) Church	___	___	___	___
12) Foreign language	___	___	___	___
13) Family near	___	___	___	___
14) Bible near	___	___	___	___
15) Shopping mall	___	___	___	___
16) Believers near	___	___	___	___
17) Telephone near	___	___	___	___
18) No phone	___	___	___	___
19) Friends	___	___	___	___
20) Hostile neighbors	___	___	___	___

Conclude with prayer that each will pray for those who live on the mission field.

Projected Results:

The students will see that life is different but not impossible. God can make the hardships bearable and living close to the Lord makes it not only possible, but wonderful.

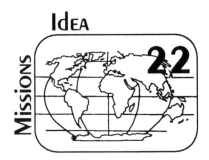

Urban Troubles

Purpose:

To help students understand that the mission field is not just the jungle and remote areas of the world, it is also large cities. The urban centers of the world have millions who need to know the Lord.

Preparation:

Cut yellow and green paper into two by four inch (2" x 4") strips. Print the names of various countries on the yellow strips and the names of major cities on the green strips. Then, write the names of missionaries you know who are serving in those cities. Before class hide the strips of paper in places around the room, in sight, but not obvious.

Supplies Needed:

Yellow and green construction paper, felt -tip pen, scissors, names of missionaries working in cities.

Time Needed:

7-8 minutes

What to do:

Have the papers prepared with countries (yellow) and cities (green). Hide those papers around the room before class begins. When it is time for the missions emphasis, divide the class into two groups. Explain that one group is to find yellow papers, the other group is to find green papers.

When all the papers are found, the yellow team must

find the correct green papers: matching the cities with the countries. If you have missionaries from your church in those countries, write their names on the green papers. Then have prayer. The teacher can begin, then pause and go around the room and each student can add the missionary and the city on the paper. Use as many or as few as you wish or add your own to the suggested list.

Yellow Papers	Green Papers
Mexico	Mexico City
South Africa	Cape Town
Venezuela	Caracas
France	Paris
Germany	Frankfurt
Nigeria	Lagos
Russia	St. Petersburg
Argentina	Buenos Aires
Columbia	Bogata
England	London
Sweden	Stockholm
Italy	Rome
Australia	Sydney
Costa Rica	San Jose
Japan	Tokyo
India	Bombay
China	Beijing
Egypt	Cairo
Holland	Amsterdam
Philippines	Manila
Vietnam	Saigon
South Korea	Seoul
Turkey	Ankara
United States	Your city and state

Projected Results:

Eyes, hearts, and minds will be opened to the concept of big city missions and the students will be aware of the "sophisticated" millions who are desperately in need of the gospel, too.

Alternative:

Use just the major cities in your country or state.

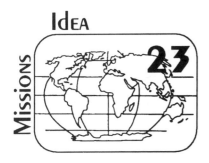

Idea

23

COUNTRY CONTEST

PURPOSE:

To familiarize the students with the world and to enjoy the process of learning about areas that need the Lord.

PREPARATION:

Locate research books, make cards with appropriate countries listed on them, display a world map with various countries outlined.

Supplies Needed:

Small cards, felt-tip pens, easel, world map, almanacs, one-volume encyclopedias, and other reference materials, pencils, paper for student notes.

Time Needed:

8-10 minutes

What to do:

On small cards, print the names of as many countries as you have students. For instance:

Kenya	Japan
Colombia	Papua New Guinea
Brazil	Cote d'Ivoire
Russia	Chile
Somalia	Poland
Peru	Canada
Australia	Spain

Place an outline map of the world on an easel. Have the outline of the countries drawn on the cards. Hand out almanacs (even a year or two old is fine), one volume encyclopedias, and whatever other books you can find to help them look up essential facts.

Ask the students to identify the country, find out three facts about the country they have been given, and the name of a missionary who serves there. (If the church knows of one in a particular country, it is most helpful if such countries are chosen.) Ask them to think of how missionaries can help with those needs and to suggest prayer requests. At the end of four minutes, ask the students, one by one, to place their country on the world map with cellophane tape or rubber cement. Conclude with a prayer session for those areas of the world.

Projected Results:

The knowledge these students acquire from personal research, from sharing with fellow students, and from adding to the world map will be helpful in adding to their missionary awareness.

Alternative:

Print the names of various states or provinces in your country. Or, you could do counties within your state. Follow the same procedures. Students will discover characteristics of "their" world and how they can serve God within familiar surroundings. Be sure to ask students to name things they can do right now, not just when they are adults.

Wiggle Out

Purpose:

To show the students that the need overseas is great, but most Christians want to stay at home.

Preparation:

Clear a place in the middle of the classroom. Become familiar with the statements to be made. Create additional ones if you wish.

Supplies Needed:

Space, five chairs, signs with the five geographic areas on them, tape, chalk

Time Needed:

5-7 minutes

What to do:

Draw a large circle with chalk on the middle of the classroom floor and write: North America. All the students must fit within the circle.

Place chairs in five different areas outside the circle. Label one Africa, one Europe, one Asia, one South America, one Asia Minor. Tape the labels to the chairs.

Explain that most Christian workers live in North America and serve there. Then make the following statements. Anyone who can answer "yes" to the first statement leaves the circle and sits in the chair for Africa. Follow the same procedure as you read each statement. Anyone who can answer "yes" to it, goes to the next vacant chair. Most of the kids will still be sitting in the North America circle when you are done.

Statement 1: If you can speak a language other than English, go sit in Africa.

Statement 2: If your birthday is today, go sit in South America.

Statement 3: If you have never been sick, go sit in Asia Minor.

Statement 4: If your mother was born in Ireland, go sit in Europe.

Statement 5: If your Bible is worn out from overuse, go sit in Asia.

Point out how few go to the places in this game, and just as few go to the foreign mission field in real life. We don't need to be "special" to go. God has called each of us to, *"Go ye therefore, and teach all nations, baptizing them in the name of the Father, and of the Son, and of the Holy Ghost: teaching them to observe all things whatsoever I have commanded you: and lo, I am with you alway, even unto the end of the world" (Matthew 28:19-20).*

Take this opportunity to stress that the opportunity and command from our Lord is that all people—adults and kids—are to be witnesses to the whole world. That "whole world" includes the kids down the block, kids on the sports team at school, sisters and brothers, and even parents.

Projected Results:

The students will get an object lesson about the imbalance of missionaries versus those who are not missionaries, either at home or abroad.

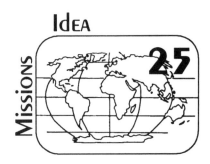

Music for Missions

Purpose:

To help the students put their thoughts about missions into words and to remember those thoughts in the future.

Preparation:

Think through a "made-up" song like the one below, and practice singing it — no matter what your voice is like. The students won't care about perfect pitch.

Supplies Needed:

Paper and pencils, piano, and someone to finger out a tune with one finger, some music for simple tunes.

Time Needed:

Approximately 10 minutes

What to do:

Select a familiar tune like "The Farmer in the Dell." Put some simple words to it like:
> "Go out and tell the world,
> Go out and tell the world,
> Hi, ho, the Bible says,
> Go out and tell the world."

Then tell the students they are to make up a missionary song to sing and obey. Suggest other tunes that might work, like: "O How I love Jesus," "Jesus Loves Me," or "London Bridge." Ask their suggestions for simple tunes.

Divide the students into teams of two or three. Each group selects a tune and then works out some words that fit correctly. They should learn to sing it and share it with the class. If they get mixed up with doctrine, help them in the small groups. If they get mixed up with notes, help them. If they struggle to accomplish a simple but meaningful ditty, work with them in their small groups. Try to put a student who is having an easy time with this in a group with those who might struggle.

After five to seven minutes, they should be ready to share with the rest of the class. Keep the songs and re-sing them for the next several weeks. You may want to arrange a special program of one or more that your students really like. Practice and sing it before the church while it is meaningful to the class and still fresh in their minds and on their lips.

Projected Results:

Students will learn a lesson about missions, even if they aren't interested. They will sing that message in class, at home, and maybe for the whole church, making the message multiply its effectiveness. Music will remain in the memory long after a lesson is forgotten.

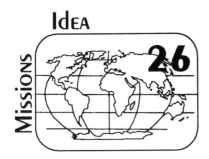

Idea

Missions

26

OVERSEAS DRAMA

PURPOSE:

To let the students get a feel for people who live in other lands and cultures.

PREPARATION:

Make a list of countries where your church has a missionary interest. Have the names of the missionaries available. Choose one of them and know something of the climate, the houses, the dress, the work of the people after the country is chosen.

Supplies Needed:

Encyclopedia, missionary magazines, prayer cards

Time Needed:

8-12 minutes

What to do:

Explain about the country chosen to dramatize. Tell about the climate, the houses, the dress, the customs of the people, the religion, if any. Show a picture of your church's missionary who serves among those people. Tell the students they are to show, via drama, how hard or easy it would be in that place to share the gospel and lead the people to Christ. Give out parts such as:

Head man   Children
Medicine man   Missionary
Chief religious leader   Local political leader
Several wives and mothers
Several husbands and fathers

Make some simple props. They can be just signs
saying: PALM TREE   LOCAL MEETING AREA
FIRE   HOME   LOCAL CHURCH/TEMPLE/MOSQUE

The drama should be impromptu. Give one person the
opening sentence. It should be something that shows
the person does not know Christ, a provocative
statement. It could go something like this:
HEAD MAN: "Who are these strangers who have come
to our village? What do they want?"

or

HEAD MAN: "My wife is very sick. The medicine man
must be called to heal her."

Then let the other students add their own comments to
the conversation, acting out life as they think it is there,
without Jesus. How would the people act and think? The
missionary should try to lead them to Christ, and the
people should come up with some objections to the
gospel. Portray some trying to hinder the missionary's
work. Let some of the adults and the children come to
Christ. Have one say "no" to Christ and turn away.

This is especially good just after a missionary from this
field has been to your church. Or, you could do it just
before a missionary comes and let the students see how
close they came to understanding the actual conditions
on that mission field.

Projected Results:

The students will probably know a mission field better
than the adults in the church do. They will see needs
that others may not realize; they will want to see the
gospel reach into that country.

Alternative:

Select a city or region of your city as the mission field.
Explain the neighborhood chosen, the kinds of people
who live there. Show pictures of people from your
church who live in that area or near it as representatives
of the missionaries. Be sure to include pictures of your
students if their neighborhoods are selected. Let
students develop an impromptu drama on how they
would witness in the city or neighborhood selected. Let
them practice how to share the gospel where there is no
language barrier.

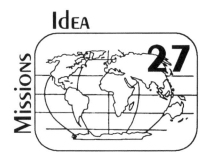

Idea

27

Missions

Excuses, Excuses

Purpose:

To help the students realize that there are innumerable excuses for not going to the mission field, for not serving the Lord, at home or abroad.

Preparation:

None

Supplies Needed:

Papers and pencils, timer or watch

Time Needed:

5 minutes

What to do:

Begin with a loud shout: "I won't! I won't go to the mission field!" Then, ask this question: "Why do most people stay home from the mission field?" Do not allow an answer. Instead, immediately, let two students give out the papers and pencils.

Then explain: "At the top of your paper write, EXCUSES, EXCUSES! In three minutes, see how many excuses you can write down on your paper about why people would not go to the mission field. See who can get the most excuses. One, two three: GO!" After three minutes, stop the class, ask them to count up their excuses.

The student with the most excuses gets to read his/her list first. Others are to add any different ones they have on their list.

Close with a prayer for people to be open to God's call which may be to stay home or which may be to go! Help the students to realize that God needs people at home to witness, pray, serve, and financially support the foreign missionaries, but that everyone should be ready and willing to go if God leads in that direction.

Projected Results:

The students will realize most excuses are phony, only a few are legitimate. They should begin to see the difference, and seek God's will for their lives. Students will also begin to realize the excuses they give for not serving God right now in their homes and schools.

Help students to realize that they are God's missionaries right now to their schools, their friends, and their families. Ask them to silently evaluate whether or not they have ever used those excuses not to witness and what they can do to change their attitudes.

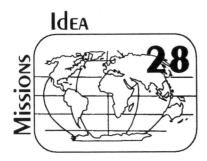

IdEA

Missions

28

Traveling for God

PURPOSE:

To see the adventure and the hardships of traveling to, from, and within the mission fields of the world.

PREPARATION:

Copy the list below. Make one per student.

Supplies Needed:

Copier and paper, blank sheets of paper, pencils

Time Needed:

5-8 minutes

What to do:

Tell the kids that travel may be easy for them, but in many areas of the world, travel is difficult. Ask two students to pass out the papers and the pencils. At the count of three, they are to do what the directions tell them. When they are finished, they bring the paper to the teacher and are given another paper to make a paper airplane they can "fly" toward a corner of the room.

TRAVELING FOR GOD
1) Draw lines from the type of transportation to the places that would use the different types of transportation listed.
2) Circle the places that would be hardest to travel in.
3) Underline the places that are easy to travel in.
4) List their favorite forms of transportation.
5) Describe the advantages of the airplane for missionary work.

RICKSHAW	Haiti
TRAIN	Germany
OCEAN LINER	United States
CAR	Peru
DONKEY	Russia
CANOE	Australia
TAXI	Kenya
BUS	China
HORSE	Philippines
BICYCLE	Argentina
TRUCK	Austria
FOOT	Spain
DOG SLED	Mongolia
AIRPLANE	Papua New Guinea
BOAT	Poland
JEEP	Colombia
DONKEY	France
	Hungary
	Egypt
	India
	Taiwan
	Japan
	Indonesia
	Venezuela
	Chad
	Italy
	Brunei
	Bolivia
	Portugal

My favorite forms of transportation would be:

_____

Advantages of the airplane for missionaries:

_____

When a student is finished, he/she turns in the finished paper and gets a piece of blank paper to make a paper airplane. Provide an area to "fly" the airplanes to while waiting for the others to complete their papers. You may want to designate various corners of the room as countries. Finally, go over the papers in class.

Projected Results:

A sense of the transportation needs missionaries have to take the gospel around the world.

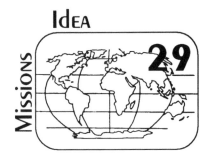

Idea
Missions
29

Missionball

Purpose:

To give the students a fun time that will encourage an openness to missions.

Preparation:

Get supplies, clear an area of the classroom or move outdoors.

Supplies Needed:

A soft foam ball, cardboard and felt-tip pens to make name tags, string and hole punch

Time Needed:

10 minutes

What to do:

Explain to the class:

"Those in the outside circle represent the world—those not interested in Jesus, the Bible, missions, or anything Christian. The three inside the circle represent those who love Jesus and want to serve Him through missions at home or abroad. Some will go, some will give, some will pray, all will witness, and, together, they will seek to reach the world for the Lord."

Choose three class members to be in the circle. All the other students form a big circle around them. The three inside must wear tags around their necks which read:

1) I'll Go.   2) I'll Give.   3) I'll Pray.

The object of those outside the circle is to stop the people in the circle from GOING, GIVING, PRAYING for missions. They are to throw the ball (like in Dodge Ball) at those in the center. The ball must be aimed at the area between the waist and the ankles. (If someone is hit by the ball above the waist or below the ankles, it doesn't count.)

If they hit one, that one must leave the circle. The game keeps going until they have hit all three, and stopped the GOING, GIVING, and PRAYING. If there is time, choose three different students to be in the center. Limit the playing to about ten minutes to avoid boredom. It can always be played again at another time. Talk about what happens when the *giving, praying,* and *going* are stopped.

Projected Results:

An active exercise that will generate enthusiasm as well as an opportunity to realize the need for GIVING and PRAYING as well as GOING. Students will see that there are people who do not want the gospel to be given to others. Talk about why this might be so and how they can be better witnesses.

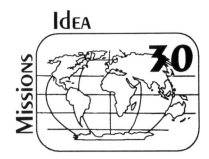

Steps Ahead

Purpose:

To encourage the students to consider the mission field and to realize that all believers are responsible to witness for the Lord, which would make them missionaries wherever they are and whatever age they are.

Preparation:

Clear out a space in the classroom and make a chalk line at both boundaries.

Supplies Needed:

Space and chalk

Time Needed:

5-6 minutes

What to do:

Ask the students to line up across the left side of the area on the chalk line. The rules are: Choose a question, answer it, and advance toward the winners' line according to the measure of the question. The first one to the line is the "winner." If there is time, continue for the second and third place "winners."

Take three shoe-long steps if you can:
1) Name a religion that does not teach about Jesus.
2) Name a missionary our church helps support.
3) Name an occupation God could use on the mission field.
4) Name a reason for not going to the mission field.

5) Name a country in South America where missionaries serve.
6) Name a way missionaries travel.
7) Name a place to study to be a missionary.
8) Name a reason for going to the mission field.
9) Name a language missionaries use.
10) Name an animal missionaries see in Africa.

Take three AS-BIG-AS-YOU-CAN steps if you can:
1) Quote a Bible verse that tells us to be missionaries.
2) Explain briefly the way to know Jesus personally as Saviour.
3) Name a missionary you have prayed for.
4) Name a missionary organization that sends out missionaries.
5) Explain one way someone can prepare for the mission field.
6) Explain one way you can be a missionary today, right where you are.
7) Name a place in North America that needs missionaries.
8) Name a missionary from past history.
9) Name what you think are the three hardest tasks of a missionary.
10) Answer, "Who was the greatest missionary in the Bible?"

Repeat each statement after they have all been asked once. Answers cannot be repeated (except #2 in BIG-AS-YOU-CAN questions, telling someone how to know Jesus personally). If students don't know the answer, they must remain where they were until the next turn. You can make up and add other statements or actions (such as hop three times).

Projected Results:

The game is fun, relaxing, and informative. The students will reveal what they know about missions, and the teacher will be able to add some teaching where it is needed. Students will see that a missionary is anyone who tells someone else about Jesus. Perhaps a week or two before playing the "STEPS AHEAD" game, some of the information can be shared with the students to make it easier for them to answer the statements.

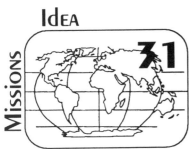

Idea 31

Missions

IF I WERE...

PURPOSE:

To help the students think through the possibility of missions in their lives.

PREPARATION:

Copy the "IF I WERE..." list: one for each student

SUPPLIES NEEDED:

Pencils, copied papers, work table

TIME NEEDED:

5-6 minutes

WHAT TO DO:

Give each student a list of the following open-ended sentences:

1) If I were a missionary, I'd like to go to..._____

_____

2) If I were rich, I would like to help..._____

_____

3) If I were ready to graduate from high school, I'd like to...

_____

4) If I were to hear a missionary speak about a difficult place to serve God, I would like to...

_____

5) If I earned some money, I would like to send some of it to...

_____

6) If I were asked to go to the jungle for a month to help a missionary, I would...

_____

7) If I were a teacher, I would ask God to..._____

_____

8) If I knew Jesus is the only way of salvation and saw most people did not know this, I would...

_____

Instruct the students to choose only three of the "IF I WERE..." sentences to answer. Give them about four minutes to write out the answers, and then let them share what they wrote. There are no right or wrong answers. You are looking for honesty. The discussion starters in the answers will enable you to observe what the attitudes of the students are. Praise them for their work and pray for their commitment to missions at home and far away—and to personal holiness in their day by day Christian living.

Projected Results:

A new awareness of personal responsibility; a desire to serve God both now and in the future.

Add-A-Line

Purpose:

To encourage creativity and honesty and to let the students voice opinions in a creative writing exercise.

Preparation:

Copy the "ADD-A-LINE" section, one per student. Think through a sample that would help the students to be able to make up their own.

Supplies Needed:

Copier, pencils, work table

Time Needed:

5-6 minutes, more or less as your class shows interest

What to do:

Give out the papers with this ADD-A-LINE:

Because people are lost without Jesus,
Because people are hungry for food and faith,
Because people are living in sin and need to know that there is a better life, I will...

_____

_____

_____.

Ask the students to finish the "ADD-A-LINE" by completing the paper and to be ready to share their ending with the class. When they are finished, place the "ADD-A-LINEs" on the bulletin board, if the students don't mind, or send them home. Praise them for trying and pray for those in your class who are without Christ as well as those around the world.

Then, ask the students to open their Bibles to Acts 1:8 and read it in unison. Divide the class into groups and alternate saying it. An easy division is at the punctuation marks. Go around the groups and then switch groups.

"But ye shall receive power, after that the Holy Ghost is come upon you: and ye shall be witnesses unto me both in Jerusalem, and in all Judaea, and in Samaria, and unto the uttermost part of the earth."

Talk about what the verse means and where their "Jerusalem," "Judaea," "Samaria," and "uttermost part of the earth" might be. Remind students that Samaria was a place the Jews did not want to go. They hated the Samaritans.

Projected Results:

A growing desire in the students' hearts to share the gospel with those who don't have the advantages they have. Students will also learn a new memory verse which will help them remember that witnessing is missions and it begins at home, in nearby areas, and then goes into the world.

Idea 33

Missions

Exam for Life

Purpose:

To help students to think about their future and to allow God to lead them into His choice for their life work.

Preparation:

Make enough copies of the EXAM FOR LIFE so that each student and visitor can have one

Supplies Needed:

Copier, work table, pens

Time Needed:

6-8 minutes one class, 6-8 minutes the next class

What to do:

Explain to the students that the "EXAM FOR LIFE" is very important—not to the teacher but to each student. There are no right or wrong answers. They will not be graded on the exam. But it is very personal and needs their undivided attention and honesty. Pass out the "EXAMS FOR LIFE." Pray for the students as they answer the questions, and let them begin their work. Be prepared to help them, but do not answer any questions for them.

EXAM FOR LIFE

1) My full name:_____

2) My age:_____

3) My grade in school: _____

4) My favorite subject in school: _____

5) My favorite television program: _____

6) I like to read: _____

7) My top two ambitions for the future:

_____

8) Would I like to go to college? Yes_____   No_____

9) What kind of career work would I like to do?

_____

10) What talents do I have?

_____

_____

_____

How did I get the talents and abilities I have?

_____

Why do I have those abilities and talents?

_____

_____

11) Could God use my talents?_____

How?_____

_____

12) Am I willing to let God use my talents?

_____

13) Will I consider missionary work if God calls me?

_____

14) Am I willing to consider the foreign mission field? ___

15) Will I serve God at home?_____

16) How will I know where God wants me?_____

_____

_____

17) Choose a Bible verse that you will use to guide your future choices.

_____

_____

18) Does God want everyone to go overseas to the mission field?

_____

19) Does God want me on the foreign mission field?

_____

20) How can I be a missionary today?

_____

_____

Projected Results:

An open mind toward global missions; a willingness to discuss the pros and cons; a desire to be available as a "home-front" missionary now and in the future; an awareness that their abilities are gifts from God that rightfully belong to Him for His use.

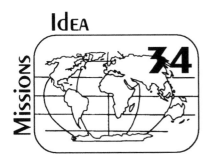

IDEA

34

Missions

GUESS-WHAT?

PURPOSE:

To continue developing missions awareness in the students.

PREPARATION:

Make a circle of chairs; list countries and needs

SUPPLIES NEEDED:

Chairs

TIME NEEDED:

10 minutes

WHAT TO DO:

Have the class sit in a circle. The teacher stands in the middle of the circle and begins the following by being "IT":

"IT" says, "Guess-what, Jane?"
JANE answers, "What?"
IT: "There's a need."
JANE: "Where?"
IT: "In Argentina."
JANE: "What's the need?"
IT: "The people need to know Jesus."
JANE: "What can I do about it?"
IT: "You can pray."

IT then writes: PRAY FOR ARGENTINA on the chalkboard. Jane becomes "IT" and starts the conversation again. Use the same routine until "IT" gets to answer "Where?" Jane changes the location and the need, which could be for food, more support, for more missionaries, for Christians to be baptized, for people to read the Bible, etc.

The teacher should list known needs or general needs on a paper to help "IT" select countries and needs as necessary. Then "IT" writes the need on the chalkboard. "IT" should not select a student who has already had a turn to answer the "GUESS-WHAT." At the end of the allotted time, stop and pray for the needs. Ask each student to select a need from those listed, and pray audibly or silently for that need.

Projected Results:

Developing missions consciousness as well as a mentally challenging opportunity for class participation.

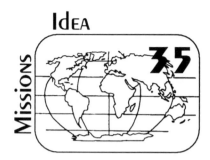

Bible-less

PURPOSE:

To help the students see how the Bible has influenced our whole lives and how different life would be without it.

PREPARATION:

Gather supplies

SUPPLIES NEEDED:

Papers, pencils, work table

TIME NEEDED:

6-7 minutes

WHAT TO DO:

Ask two students to hand out papers and pencils. They should print across the top: BIBLE-LESS: NO BIBLE, NO?

Explain that at the count of three, they are to list as many places, activities, things, and celebrations that would not exist if Christ had not come and there were no Bible to tell us about Him.

Tell the class to try to name 20 ideas. After three or four minutes, even if no one has reached 20, stop. Let the student with the most items on his/her list, read it to the others. Others can fill in with different items from their lists.

To get them started, mention:
Christmas
Churches
Hospitals

Finally, point out that there are still Bible-less people in many parts of the world who need missionaries. Quote Luke 10:2: *"Therefore said he unto them, the harvest truly is great, but the labourers are few: pray ye therefore the Lord of the harvest, that he would send forth labourers into his harvest."*

PRAY for those Bible-less people! Discuss what harvest the verse is talking about. List ways your students can be labourers now as well as in the future. Ask why Jesus said the "labourers are few."

Projected Results:

A new awareness of how deeply Christianity has affected their everyday lives and enjoyments; a keener interest in seeing the gospel of the Lord Jesus get to those who have never heard; a new sense that there are those around us every day who don't have a Bible and know nothing about it.

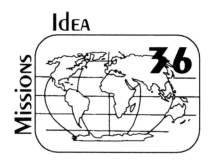

MONEY LOVE

PURPOSE:

To show how important money is to the work of the Lord around the world.

PREPARATION:

Get supplies

Supplies Needed:

Work table, play money, basket, paper and pencils

Time Needed:

6–8 minutes

What to do:

Pass out play money to the students, perhaps $10,000 each. Play the following two games with them:

MISSIONARY NEEDS
As they hear of the needs, they put their money into a basket in the center of the table. Point out that these are not all the expenses a missionary has, but these amounts for needs are examples. Actually, there are many more needs, especially if the missionary is married and has children. Do they need our prayers!

1) Transportation: $1500.00
2) Housing: $1000.00
3) Food: $70 per week x 52 weeks = $3640
4) Language study: $950
5) Jeep (one year's expenses): $1,013
6) Literature (Bibles and booklets): $541

7) Office supplies: $267
8) Health, life and car Insurance: $1,080

Balance: $9.00

MY MONEY
Give each $1,000 and let them "spend it" in whatever ways they wish. It should be a yearly expenditure. As they do, have them place their money into the basket in the center of the table and write the amounts down on scrap paper as they go along.

Per year I will spend:
For God: _____   For snack foods: _____
For new clothes: _____   For trips: _____
For recreational equipment (bicycle, skates, etc): _____
Gifts for family and friends: _____
For admission to concerts, sporting events: _____
For extras that come up: _____
(Realistically, many children, especially younger ones who do not have jobs or babysit, wouldn't have $1,000 per year. Rather, they probably get a weekly allowance, but the principle would apply.)

Explain at the end that most people give too much for their own needs and not enough for God. Ask them to divide the money they gave to God's work into local church needs and missions needs. Young people may wish to give all to the mission field, but point out that if there were no home church, there would be no missionaries. It would be a good time to point out that God suggests 10 percent for Himself as a minimum, with an offering besides.

Projected Results:

The students will begin to get an idea of what it costs to keep a missionary on a foreign field as well as begin to see the need for personal budgeting and on wise spending that includes giving to God what He desires.

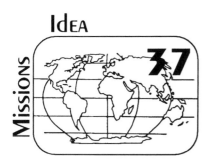

IdEa

Missions

37

Who's Great

Purpose:

To allow the students to see that, *"...Man looketh on the outward appearance, but the Lord looketh on the heart"* (I Samuel 16:7). It is better to serve the Lord, even on a remote mission field, than to have great fame as a president, performer, or artist.

Preparation:

Write the verse on a chalkboard or posterboard. Copy the list of occupations given below—one per student.

Supplies Needed:

Copier, chalkboard and chalk or posterboard and felt-tip pen, pencils, work table

Time Needed:

Approximately 4-6 minutes

What to do:

Distribute the following list to the students. Ask them to put a number beside each occupation and rank its importance: On the left side for man's opinion, on the right side for God's opinion. Let #1 be the highest, #10 the lowest.

Man's Opinion		God's Opinion
____	Doctor	____
____	Minister	____
____	Carpenter	____
____	Lawyer	

Man's Opinion		God's Opinion
____	Plumber	____
____	President	____
____	Writer	____
____	Mayor	____
____	Missionary	____

There are no concrete rules, just personal views. When they are finished, ask someone to read "man's opinion" and someone else to read "God's opinion." Remind the students that being a missionary isn't necessarily #1. Being what *God wants* us to be is #1. Talk about why the world views these occupations one way and God might look at them another.

Finally, ask them to memorize I Samuel 16:7b: *"...for man looketh on the outward appearance, but the Lord looketh on the heart."* One effective way to do this is to divide the class into two teams: one side of the room is #1; the other side is #2. Side #1 says: "...For Man looketh on the outward appearance," the other side responds, "...but the Lord looketh on the heart". Repeat it three times and then reverse the parts. Finally, let them all say the entire phrase, along with the reference.

Another option is to go around the circle with each person adding the next word (or two words) in the verse. When you've gone around two or three times, everyone should have had an opportunity to say different parts of the verse.

Projected Results:

The students should realize that fame and fortune should not be their chief aim in life. Serving the Lord and becoming a man or woman of God is far more important. They can serve Him through one of those occupations or in some other way, but it all depends on their motives — are they doing it for money and position or for God.

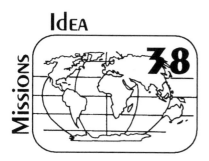

All Play?—No Way

Purpose:

To show the students that working for the Lord, at home or abroad, is not all play. It is hard work and requires the strength and wisdom of God.

Preparation:

No advance preparation

Supplies Needed:

A spinner, chalkboard, chalk, prize

Time Needed:

6-7 minutes

What to do:

The students can sit around a table to play the game. Begin with the child to the left of the teacher and continue clockwise around the circle. The player spins the spinner and if the spinner lands on an even number, the child must tell an easy way to serve Jesus here, in their home town.

If the spinner lands on an odd number, the child must tell: A hard part in serving Jesus here in our home town. No answer can be repeated.

Give the student the number of points indicated when the spinner stops if he/she can give a different hard or easy part of serving Jesus within ten seconds. Keep score on the chalkboard.

After three minutes, change the answers. If the spinner lands on an even number, the students must give an easy way to serve God on the foreign mission field.

If the spinner lands on an odd number, the student tells a *hard* part of serving God on the foreign mission field. After another three minutes, add up the scores and pronounce a winner. Have a small prize for the winner—perhaps a game from another country or cookies from a foreign country.

Close with prayer, asking that each student will enjoy serving the Lord and not be afraid of the difficulties. Also, pray for the missionaries they are familiar with for the sacrifices they make to serve the Lord and for His strength through hard times.

Projected Results:

The students will learn to be imaginative and think realistically about serving the Lord—the blessings and the difficulties. They will learn to pay attention so they do not repeat the same phrase as another student.

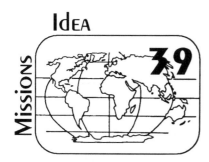

IdEA

Missions

39

IMAGINE

Purpose:

To help the students "IMAGINE" what the work of the Lord is like around the world and at home.

Preparation:

Copy the IMAGINE situations

Supplies Needed:

Copier, paper

Time Needed:

8-10 minutes

What to do:

Write the "IMAGINE" skits on separate sheets of paper.

1) IMAGINE: You are saying good-bye to your family and leaving for Asia as a missionary.

2) IMAGINE: You are witnessing to your best friend about Jesus.

3) IMAGINE: You are at prayer meeting praying for a foreign missionary as he/she helps a sick person.

4) IMAGINE: You are deciding what career to follow for your life's work.

5) IMAGINE: You are trying to learn a foreign language to be effective as a missionary.

6) IMAGINE: You are teaching a Bible verse to children in a younger department.

7) IMAGINE: You are leading a service at a nursing home to share Jesus and His love with the elderly.

8) IMAGINE: You are inviting some friends to Sunday School and church.

9) IMAGINE: You are traveling through the jungle in order to take the gospel to people far from anywhere.

10) IMAGINE: You are asked to give money for a missionary project that needs many dollars.

Divide the class into three groups and appoint a captain for each group. Place the pile of "IMAGINE" skits on a table. The captain from Team 1 comes up, takes a skit, and shows it to his/her team. The group then acts out what is suggested and the other students try to guess what is going on. The first person on another team to guess correctly wins the opportunity for their team to do the next skit.

PROJECTEd REsulTs:

As the students put themselves into the roles of missionaries and witnesses for the Lord, it will be a step toward spiritual growth and becoming what God wants them to be.

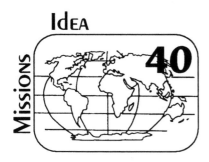

Idea 40

Paths Far Away

Purpose:

To give students board game fun with an indirect teaching about missions that they may never forget.

Preparation:

Make a board game including the cards

Supplies Needed:

Heavy cardboard approximately 30 inches square, assorted felt markers, index cards, assorted buttons, spinner, playing table

Time Needed:

15 minutes or more (This game could be played for eight minutes or so each week for a period of several weeks.)

What to do:

Place the game board in the center of the table. It should have a long path drawn from **START** to the **END** in the farthest corner. Draw some attractive pictures or use magazine picture cut-outs to make the path look exciting. Divide the path into 1 inch squares. Leave some spaces on the path blank. On others write such words as:

Exchange places with someone   Take a triangle card
Take a rectangle card   Advance One space
Go back to the beginning   Advance three spaces
Advance to a yellow square   Take an extra turn
Advance to a red square   Lose a turn

Go back to a blue square   Advance two spaces
Move two squares behind   Draw a square card
   your closest opponent

On the rectangle cards print these words:
1) How can a child be a missionary?
2) Name someone you know who needs Jesus.
3) Quote a Bible verse.
4) Explain the importance of Sunday School.
5) How can a child use his/her voice for Jesus?
6) How could you help a sick adult?

On the square cards write:
1) What is a missionary?
2) How can I know if God wants me to be a missionary?
3) Where is there a big need for missionaries?
4) Read Matthew 28:19-20.
5) Name a missionary you know personally.
6) Name two countries where your church has missionaries.

On the triangle cards write:
1) Tell how to pray for missions work.
2) Tell what Jesus says is important about witnessing.
3) Tell how we can give more to missions.
4) Tell when is a good time to pray for missions.
5) Tell when we can start being missionaries.
6) Tell how to be a missionary to your sports team.

Projected Results:

Most children enjoy board games and this one will provide fun, relaxing learning about missions as well as an opportunity for the teacher to see the attitudes and knowledge of the students in a non-threatening way.

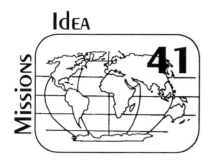

IdEA

Missions

41

No Arguments

Purpose:

To help the students realize that they must not argue against God. He wants each of His children to serve Him, one way or another.

Preparation:

Make a bean bag target approximately two by three feet from a carton or cardboard box. If you would like to get better acquainted with one or two of the students, ask them to help you during the week. Cut four separate circles out of the top side of the carton which are big enough for the bean bag to go through easily. Label the circles: 1, 2, 3, 4. Write: "NO ARGUMENTS" in large letters on the sides of the carton. (If you prefer, you could draw circles on the cardboard, label them, and have a Bean Bag Toss that lands on the circle rather than going into a hole.)

Supplies Needed:

A carton approximately 2' x 3', sharp scissors or utility knife, felt-tip pens, bean bag, paper and pen for scorekeeping, chalk, empty space

Time Needed:

10-12 minutes

What to do:

Place the Bean Bag Target at one end of the room. Ask the students to line up behind a chalk line ten feet away. One student at a time throws a bean bag toward the target.

If the bean bag lands in "circle 1," the student tells one reason why he/she loves Jesus and gets 200 points.

If the bean bag lands in "circle 2," the student gives one reason to tell a friend about Jesus and gets 150 points.

If the bean bag lands in "circle 3," the student gives one suggestion for helping a foreign missionary and gets 125 points.

If the bean bag lands on "circle 4," the student tells one reason to memorize Scripture and gets 175 points.

If the bean bag lands outside the circles, the student must give one reason for not witnessing for Jesus and loses 25 points.

If time allows, go through the group of students twice. Do not prolong the game indefinitely, but reuse it a few weeks later. Answers can only be given once. Students cannot duplicate another student's response.

PROjECTEd REsulTs:

Students will have to think quickly about reasons to witness and why. They will develop a keener knowledge of the Lord's call to witness and help others who are witnessing both at home and around the world.

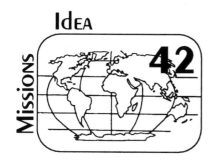

Idea

Missions

42

Love Action

Purpose:

To let the students serve as missionaries now.

Preparation:

Make a list of possible missionary projects like the one listed below. Announce the LOVE ACTION several weeks before the actual project.

Supplies Needed:

Will depend on the project chosen. Be prepared! If the students will be off the church property, permission slips are important. Parents should be aware of the project from the beginning and encouraged to participate with transportation or other needs.

Time Needed:

3-4 minutes to select a project, "LOVE ACTION DAY" may take hours.

What to do:

Make a list of three or four possible ministries. Some possible LOVE ACTION activities:

1) Put on a service at a nursing home.
2) Help cut grass and clean up the yard of an elderly or sick person.
3) Help one Sunday in the church nurseries.
4) Put on a Christian play for a group of seniors.
5) Select a neighborhood near the church and place tracts at front doors or pass them out on a street corner downtown.

6) Make up a letter to write to friends who don't know Jesus and print it neatly. Mail it to two friends.
7) Help at a downtown mission or another one of your church's outreach programs.

Let the students vote on what they want and can do as a project together. Perhaps two projects could be attempted. Make all the plans necessary (arrangements with the nursing home or the senior center, buying tracts, securing an easy-to-produce play or puppet program (*Dramatic Readings for All Occasions* or *The Adventures of Moses* are two possibilities), or whatever other advance preparation needs to be done. Announce the project for two or three weeks in advance and pray with the students for the project. Remind them this is "missionary" work, too.

Projected Results:

A taste for Christian service should result in a desire for more. Most children like to help and need to feel that they are important to God and His work, too. Make it possible for them to continue to serve in special places. Praise their good work and encourage them to look for other ways to serve God.

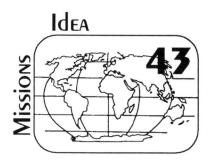

Idea 43

Missions

Tag Out

Purpose:

To have fun with a missions emphasis; a change of pace.

Preparation:

Clear the room of chairs. Make or buy small flags of as many different countries around the world as you can find. Put them on craft sticks. Have more flags than there are students. Blow up a large balloon, draw a large Bible on it and put it on a two foot ribbon.

Supplies Needed:

Large balloon, two feet of ribbon, felt-tipped pens, small flags (purchased or drawn—old almanacs have flags in them that could be cut out), craft sticks, vase or other container, open space

Time Needed:

10 minutes

What to do:

Select a student to be "IT." Explain that IT carries the Bible-balloon and tries to tag any other student in the room. To avoid too much noise and running, try a WALKING TAG. The student who holds the Bible-balloon is IT. IT chases any student with a flag and tries to tag him/her. When IT tags someone, he/she shouts:

*"Go **YE** into all the world, and preach the gospel to every creature" (Mark 16:15).*

The child who is tagged becomes IT and takes the

Bible-balloon, waits until the Bible verse is finished, counts to ten and starts chasing the other students.

The former IT takes the flag from the one he/she tagged, calls out the country whose flag he/she has, and places it in a vase. This person stays out of the TAG OUT for 60 seconds or until a new player becomes IT. Then he gets a new flag and re-enters the game.

After eight minutes, call "time" and ask the students to call out the flags that were "reached" and are now in the vase. Point out the need to take the Bible to every one of those countries and show the people their need for Christ. Ask the students to repeat Mark 16:15 in unison once more, and close that part of the class with a prayer for missions.

Play this game again in a few weeks. Don't repeat it too often; it will lose its effect.

Projected Results:

This new game will offer special fun and an opportunity to learn the names of other countries of our world. The emphasis on YE in the verse will help each to sense a personal responsibility to spread the gospel.

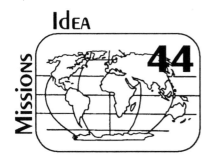

IdEA

Missions

44

This and That

Purpose:

To teach the students to talk about serious things like knowing Jesus Christ as Saviour and serving God through telling others about Him.

Preparation:

Print the sayings on slips of paper and fold them in half.

Supplies Needed:

Small pieces of paper, perhaps 4 x 6 inches, pen or typewriter.

Time Needed:

7-8 minutes ought to be enough

What to do:

Place the folded slips of paper on the center of the table. Explain to the students the process. "We all talk about THIS AND THAT. Let's see if we discover ways to let God turn our conversations around to be a witness for Him. I will begin this game. I will pick up a slip of paper and use the sentence to begin a conversation with an imaginary person. The object is to turn the conversation from its topic to a witness for Christ. When I finish (in 60 seconds) the student to my left will take the next paper and do the same. We will continue around the room."

The papers can say the following conversation openers:
1) "Isn't the weather beautiful?"
2) "I didn't do too well on that test."

3) "My mother is mad at me."
4) "I'm sorry you have been sick."
5) "Are you going to the party?"
6) "What are you going to do on the weekend?"
7) "I love to read."
8) "Are you a baseball fan?"
9) "What's your favorite TV show?"
10) "Let's go to McDonald's."
11) "Do you play the piano?"
12) "What's the date?"
13) "Bike riding is so much fun."
14) "I need some new clothes."
15) "That new song is awesome."
16) "I've got to clean my room."
17) "What's for supper?"
18) "If I were president, I'd change things."
19) "My teacher doesn't like me."
20) "Football is the most exciting thing in the world."

Be careful not to condemn any attempt by the students. If they struggle, help them to find the right words.

Projected Results:

The students will feel more comfortable about talking about Jesus after practicing in class. They will see ways they can lead a conversation naturally into spiritual topics. Encourage them. Show them that they are missionaries serving the Lord every time they tell someone about Jesus.

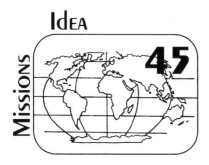

IDEA
Missions

45

ANIMAL RACE

PURPOSE:

To help the students be missionaries right in their own community as they bring friends to hear about Jesus.

PREPARATION:

Make a colorful contest board with tracks for the animals to run on. Rule it off in one inch spaces to the finish line. Make invitations for the students to hand to people they wish to invite. They could read something like this:

COME TO OUR SUNDAY SCHOOL CLASS!
IT IS INTERESTING, FUN, AND HELPFUL.
Date: _____
Time: _____
Place: _____
Invitation from: _____

Supplies Needed:

Large piece of cardboard or mural paper at least thirty by forty-two inches (30" x 42"), felt pens of varied colors, magazine cut-outs of animals, plastic animals from a child's zoo collection, table for display, copier, paper.

Time Needed:

One month, 5-7 minutes per class period

What to do:

Divide the class into teams of two or three students each. Assign them an animal (or let them choose). Have the animals along the left side of the contest board which is the starting line. Announce the ANIMAL RACE one week prior to the beginning of the contest.

Explain, "There are many people in the world who don't know Jesus and don't come to hear about Him in church. We want you to be a missionary and bring some of them in. Every time you bring someone in during the next four weeks, your team gets to color five inches on your track of the mural. If you bring five visitors, you get to color 25 inches. So get to work; help your team to WIN!"

Provide the invitations for the students and tell them you have names of those who might come, and they can see you afterward, if they would like them. (Have a list of prospects ready from adults who have visited the church, but most students will reach into their own group of friends.) On the closing day of the contest, praise everyone for trying and give a small prize to the winning team, like a bookmark or a pencil.

Help new members or visitors to feel welcome by making them part of the team whose member invited them. Let them know they are not just a statistic, but now they can invite others to come and help color in their team's ANIMAL TRACK.

Projected Results:

Students will enjoy inviting their friends and seeing the colorful trail of "inches" grow; many will develop a burden for those who don't come to class and want them to come so they can know the Lord.

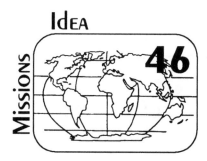

IDEA

Missions

46

MAP OUT

PURPOSE:

> To help the students see the world (and their neighborhood) as a mission field.

PREPARATION:

> Make a large outline map of the world, then make a small map of the world and have it copied so each student can have one.

Supplies Needed:

> Large piece of paper (perhaps 24" x 30") for outline map, a map or globe of the world, felt pens, easel or bulletin board for display, copier, maps to copy from, a list of church missionaries and countries where they serve, pencils, crayons or markers for the students to share.

Time Needed:

> 12-15 minutes

What to do:

> Show the large map of the world and, with the students' help, add the names of your church's missionaries in their proper countries. Then pass out the small maps and ask the students to fill in their own maps. Let them color them with pencils, crayons, or markers.
>
> Finally, ask one student who prints clearly to print on the top of the big map: "OUR MISSIONARY PRAYER MAP." Have all students do the same for their small maps to take home.

On the bottom of the map, print:
> "How then shall they call on him in whom they have not believed? and how shall they believe in him of whom they have not heard? and how shall they hear without a preacher?"

As the children leave the class, hand them their small maps and let your parting words be: "Don't forget to pray for our missionaries!"

Projected Results:

A clearer understanding of the local church missionary program, a prayer reminder for class and another one for home.

Alternative:

The same thing can be done with a map of your country or your state. Look for missionaries and mission groups which serve in these areas if your church does not have many. If you use a map of your city, you could have the students locate their streets and color in their neighborhoods with their names as the missionaries.

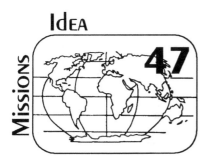

IdEA

Missions

47

Ifs and Buts

Purpose:

To enable the students to think through some ideas about the Lord and His work.

Preparation:

Copy the IFS AND BUTS

Supplies Needed:

Copier, paper, pencils

Time Needed:

8 minutes, approximately

What to do:

Explain that the students must finish each statement in five or six words. They are to complete the sentences according to God's Word, and the way they believe God would have them think.

IFS

1) If my friend doesn't know Jesus, I should...

_____

2) If a missionary needs more money to go overseas, I should...

_____

3) If the church has a missions conference, I should…

_____

4) If I feel God wants me to be a missionary, I should…

_____

5) If a missionary speaks at church, I should…

_____

BUTS
1) But my friends will laugh if I tell them about Jesus, so I should…

_____

2) But I'm too scared to be a missionary, so I should…

_____

3) But I'm too busy to go to a missions conference, so I should…

_____

4) But I want to be a lawyer, so I should…

_____

5) But I love my home too much, so I should…

_____

Collect the papers and read some of the answers— without revealing who wrote what! Discuss the answers that week or the following week (if time is short).

Projected Results:

The students will have to think through their IFS AND BUTS in relation to God and His will for their lives.

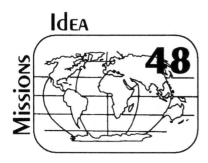

IdEA

48

COUNTRY HUNT

PURPOSE:

To help the students become better acquainted with their church's missionaries.

PREPARATION:

Obtain a list of your church's missionaries and the places in which they serve. Be sure to include any Inner-city missionaries or local Rescue Mission workers your church supports. Copy the list of missionaries and places of service.

Supplies Needed:

Copier and paper, pencils

Time Needed:

4-5 minutes

What to do:

Explain, "We're going to match the missionaries our church supports with their fields of service. Beside the name of each missionary, place the letter of the place where they serve. Their prayer cards or last letter is up front if you need to look any of them up." (Or, if you have done Idea 46, you can have them refer to the map with the names on it for help.)

COUNTRY HUNT
1) Roger and Lois Luce ____   a) Philippines
2) Bill and Mary-Ellen Stroup ____   b) Kenya
3) Ann Young ____   c) Italy
4) Judy Crossman ____   d) Venezuela

5) Jamie and Pete Zickafoos ____
6) Brian and Nancy Hoffman ____
7) Bob and Sharon Smith____
8) Lucy Aiken ____
9) Frank and Charlotte Mecklenburg ____
10) Dick and Betty Mills ____
11) Dave and Denise Flannery
12) Vince and Cathy Costa ____
13) Tom and Heather Davis____

e) Appalachia
f) Papua New Guinea
g) Qatar
h) Brazil
i) Thailand
j) Peru
k) Navajo Indian Reservation Arizona
l) Cote d'Ivoire (Ivory Coast) West Africa
m) Mid-Town Rescue Mission

Be sure to go over the answers, and pray for the missionaries as a class. You may want to assign one missionary to each student. Begin to pray and pause for each one to mention the name and the place of service of their missionary. The teacher can finish the prayer. It could be like this:

Dear Lord, we come before you to pray for our missionaries by name: ____, ____, ____, ____, ____, ____, ____. We ask that you will meet their needs, and, if possible, that you will use us to do so. We pray in Jesus' name. Amen.

Projected Results:

A real concern for those serving God in many areas of the world; a renewed awareness of the names of the missionaries their church supports; an increased sense of personal involvement in this aspect of the church; a knowledge that they can be an avenue God can use to help fulfill the needs of people who are not just anonymous missionaries, but real people.

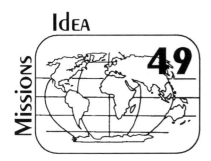

Idea

Missions

49

Joshua—Near or Far

Purpose:

To help students see that "missions" is not NEAR or FAR, it just means serving the Lord and building His church wherever He calls us.

Preparation:

Make a circle of chairs.

Supplies Needed:

Space for a circle of chairs

Time Needed:

Approximately 8-10 minutes

What to do:

Have the students sit in a circle. Have someone read Joshua 24:15: *"Choose you this day whom ye will serve; ...but as for me and my house, we will serve the Lord."* The person who is JOSHUA points to someone and says either "SERVE THE LORD—NEAR" or "SERVE THE LORD—FAR" then counts to ten.

If the student pointed at can name a place (town, city, state or province) NEAR to serve the Lord before the count of ten, all is well. But if he/she cannot, then, that student becomes the next JOSHUA and the previous JOSHUA gets to sit in the circle with the other children and teacher. JOSHUA can repeat the "SERVE THE LORD: NEAR" or can change the phrase to say: "SERVE THE LORD: FAR. One, two, three, four, five, six, seven, eight, nine, ten." The next child pointed to must say a foreign country before JOSHUA gets to ten. JOSHUA can count as fast as he or she wants.

A place NEAR is a town, city, state or province. A place FAR is a foreign country, but none can be repeated. Therefore, the students must listen carefully. The teacher is the judge and could be JOSHUA at the beginning of the game.

Try to keep the pace fast, to keep up the interest. Have the student who is JOSHUA point to a student and say: "SERVE THE LORD: NEAR" or "SERVE THE LORD: FAR" as quickly as possible and not let the game get boring.

When the game concludes, you may want to have everyone say, "We choose to serve the Lord!" You may also want to divide the class into two groups. Have one group stand up and read Joshua 24:15. Then have the second group read Joshua 24:16. Then have everyone (or a third group) read Joshua 24:24.

Projected Results:

The students will get another reminder of missions—from nearby towns and cities to faraway countries. They will also see that they must choose to follow the Lord and serve Him. They will also gain new insight into the meaning of Joshua's question to Israel.

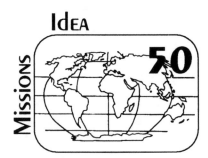

IdEA

50

Job Pursuit

Purpose:

To encourage the students to think ahead to the time when they will be ready to assume an adult role in God's plan for their lives. (This idea is not applicable for use with very young children.)

Preparation:

Copy the JOB PURSUITS

Supplies Needed:

Copier and paper, pencils

Time Needed:

10-12 minutes

What to do:

Quote Psalm 37:5 to the class: *"Commit thy way unto the Lord; trust also in him; and he shall bring it to pass."* Hand out the job pursuit form to the students and ask them to fill it out. After a few minutes, ask anyone who wishes to share some of their feelings.

JOB PURSUITS

Name _____

Grade in School _____

Three careers you might choose when you are older:

1) _____ 2) _____ 3) _____

Which one do you think you would enjoy the most?

_____

Why?_____

Which would be the best way for you to serve God?

_____

What education would these careers require?

1) _____

2) _____

3) _____

What courses can you take now that might be helpful for these careers?

1) _____

2) _____

3) _____

Which career fits best with the talents God has given you?_____

In choosing a future career, should you try to please:
Parents _____ God _____ Self _____ Friends _____?

What is the most important thing to do now as you think about your future "JOB PURSUITS?"_____

_____

Where can you get help in selecting your future "JOB PURSUIT"? _____

Does it matter how you spend your life and career?____
Why?_____

Finally, place the "JOB PURSUITS" in envelopes, seal them, ask students to write their names, the year, and the date ten years ahead. Suggest they take these envelopes home and put them away until that date ten years from now, to open and see what God has done with and for them. Print the Bible verse on the envelopes for them to remember what they did in class.

Projected Results:

A conscious desire to seek God's help in the choice of a career and to make his/her primary life's goal to do something and be someone pleasing to Him!

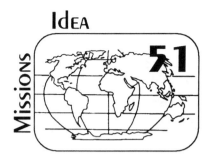

VERSE SEARCH

PURPOSE:

To show the students the fact that God is interested in all nations of the world. His desire is that each person in the world will come to know Jesus as Saviour.

PREPARATION:

None (unless you wish to add more verses or different verses to the list below)

Supplies Needed:

Chalkboard and chalk, list of missionary-oriented verses

Time Needed:

5-7 minutes

What to do:

This is a game. The students will have fun while they learn. Ask the boys and girls to place their Bibles, closed, in front of them on the table with their hands folded on top of them. The teacher calls out the Bible verse twice and says: "VERSE SEARCH, GO." The children pick up their Bibles and hunt for the verse as quickly as possible. When they find it, they stand. The first one up reads it when the teacher recognizes him/her. Allow about half the class to find the verse before calling on the winner to read. If the same person finds it first most of the time, select a second or third person to find it and read. Keep score (perhaps the boys against the girls or any other team concept). Congratulate everyone for trying and give a loud applause for the winning team.

VERSE SEARCH

1) JOHN 3:16

2) ROMANS 3:23

3) II CORINTHIANS 4:3

4) JOHN 4:42

5) MATTHEW 28:19

6) MARK 16:15

7) PSALM 22:27

8) ISAIAH 49:6

9) ISAIAH 6:8

10) LUKE 24:47

11) COLOSSIANS 1:23

12) ISAIAH 52:10

13) JOHN 15:16

14) ROMANS 10:13

15) COLOSSIANS 1:6

16) MATTHEW 1:21

17) ROMANS 1:16

18) JOHN 6:33

If a student opens the Bible before the word "GO," he/she is disqualified for that verse, but is eligible for the next "VERSE SEARCH." If some are too good at the "VERSE SEARCH," after a few times ask one quick student to be the scorekeeper and one quick student to call out the verses. That will encourage the slower ones to keep trying, rather than feel they don't have a chance.

Projected Results:

Increased familiarity with the Word of God, its books, and its contents, especially the verses about spreading the gospel.

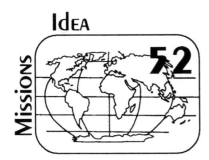

Missions Snare

Idea 52

Missions

Purpose:

To plant God's Word into the hearts of the students

Preparation:

Print the Bible verse on the chalkboard for the first week. Copy the "MISSIONS SNARE" for the second week.

Supplies Needed:

Copier, copy paper, chalkboard, chalk, eraser, pens

Time Needed:

5 minutes, two weeks in succession

What to do:

Week One: Teach the Bible verse. (You may wish to add more verses to this one as a greater challenge.)
Luke 24:47: *"And that repentance and remission of sins should be preached in his name among all the nations, beginning at Jerusalem."*

Print the verse on the chalkboard so everyone can see it. Ask the class to repeat it three times. (You can vary the repetition if you wish by having them emphasize different words each time through. For instance, they might emphasize every other word one time and every third word the next time.) Then erase one word and repeat it again. Erase another word and repeat it again, continuing until the whole verse is gone. Then repeat it once again. If time permits, ask several students to say it alone. Tell them they should remember it for a game the following week. So they may want to practice it through the week.

Week Two: Give each student a copy of the "MISSIONS SNARE" and ask them to place the words to the memory verse in the proper order.

THAT   AMONG   JERUSALEM   AND   SINS

REPENTANCE   BEGINNING   IN   AND

SHOULD   REMISSION   ALL   BE   NAME

HIS   PREACHED   NATIONS   OF   AT

_____

_____

_____

_____
                                           Luke 24:47

Ask students who they can snare with the truths of this verse and why it is important to missions. Encourage them to think through its meaning. Then have them write out what it means to them.

Luke 24:47 means:_____

_____

_____

Projected Results:

The students will get prolonged exposure to a particular Bible verse and God's Word will begin to become part of their daily thoughts, making it more effective in their lives now and in the future.

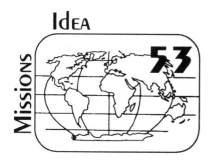

Idea

53

Missions

Need Trail

PURPOSE:

To see the needs of missionaries at home and abroad

PREPARATION:

Draw two parallel lines as a trail on the chalkboard from one corner to the other. Then divide the trail into twenty sections.

SUPPLIES NEEDED:

Chalkboard and chalk, paper (8 1/2" x 11"), pencils or pens, Gospels of John

TIME NEEDED:

Perhaps 10-12 minutes

WHAT TO DO:

Ask the students to draw a trail on their paper from one corner to the opposite corner, similar to the one drawn on the chalkboard as a sample. Every inch, draw a line across to make squares along the trail. There should be approximately 20 squares on the trail. Then, the boys and girls fill in those squares with needs that missionaries have. Make some suggestions, or encourage them to use these ideas if they wish:

money	prayer	Bibles
cars	home	clothes (for about four years)
friends	love	food

They will think of many other needs.

When they are done, they are to turn their papers over and draw a new trail on the back. Then, have them fill in the blocks with needs for missionaries in their own community. They won't need suggestions for this part. Assure them that some of the needs will be the same.

If they can fill in all the blanks, give a Gospel of John as an award, with the instruction that it is part of a missionary's equipment and they need to "pass it on."

Finish by singing the song, "Pass It On."

Projected Results:

Children will begin to think about this and see that being a servant/witness faraway or close at home doesn't change those needs. A missionary has needs that are real and necessary in the work of the Lord; many of them are the same as the ones we have every day.

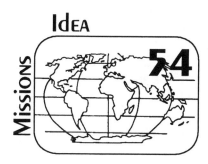

Idea

Missions

54

Jungle Board

Purpose:

To let the students think about life in the jungle

Preparation:

Use craft sticks for writing all or some of the questions below. (Call them Jungle Boards.)

Supplies Needed:

Craft sticks (or tongue depressors), fine-point felt-tip pen, basket, 3 x 5 cards or various colors of construction paper to make bookmarks

Time Needed:

8-10 minutes

What to do:

Place the Jungle Boards in a basket and hold it above the students when they select a question.

Questions to be written on JUNGLE BOARDS:
What would you do in the evening without electricity?
How would you answer a native who asks, "Isn't my god good enough"?
How would you feel if no one wrote to you while you were in the jungle?
What would you do if someone with a snake bite came to your door?
What Bible verse would you tell the people first?
How would you begin to learn the language?
If you were afraid in the jungle, name two things you could do.

How would you make friends with people in the jungle?
How would you dress in the jungle?
How could you tell people that Jesus loves them?
What would you do if you didn't like the strange foods?
What would you tell people back home in a letter?
What part of the Bible would you translate first for the jungle people?
What hymns or songs would be good to teach the people?
How could you reach the village chief?
What would you do about the bugs, spiders, wild animals, and snakes?
How would you communicate with the outside world?
Where would you pray and read your Bible?
What three books other than your Bible would you take with you into the jungle?
Who would you like to have go with you into the jungle?

Have students draw a Jungle Board out of the basket and talk about their answer for 60 seconds. When everyone has drawn at least one Jungle Board and answered the question on it, ask students for suggestions on what they can do to help their missionaries face these situations right now. List answers on the chalkboard and select one or two to carry out this week if you have time or next week if you cannot do it today.

At the end, explain to the students that those situations are very difficult and the missionaries need our prayers now. If God calls us to a foreign field as missionaries, we may have to face those same problems. But God made us a tremendous promise we can claim now and then: *"Let your conversation* [behavior] *be without covetousness; and be content with such things as ye have: for he hath said, I will never leave thee, nor forsake thee"* (Hebrews 13:5). This verse will help us to serve Him under any conditions. Have everyone write this verse down and take it home this week. You could make bookmarks with this verse on it, too, as a class project.

Projected Results:

The students will have thought through the difficulties of the mission field and realize there is a cost to serving the Lord in a remote country. They will also see a Bible truth and promise in a new light and be able to apply it in their lives now.

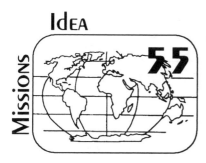

IDEA **55**

Missions

Best for You

Purpose:

To encourage the class to know and choose what is best for their lives.

Preparation:

Copy "BEST FOR YOU" SELF-TEST paper

Supplies Needed:

Copier, paper, pens

Time Needed:

10 minutes, maximum

What to do:

Give each student a copy of the self-test and a pen. Explain that the answers are to be between five and eight words. No more, no less! And, the answers are to be what is "BEST FOR YOU," no one else. Let them begin at the count of three.

"BEST FOR YOU" SELF-TEST

1) It is BEST FOR ME to tell others about Jesus when...

_____

_____

2) It is BEST FOR ME to obey my parents in...

_____

_____

3) It is BEST FOR ME to study…

_____

_____

4) It is BEST FOR ME to consider missions by…

_____

_____

5) Is is BEST FOR ME to read my Bible daily at…

_____

_____

6) It is BEST FOR ME to memorize Bible verses while…

_____

_____

7) It is BEST FOR ME to live a good life for Jesus by…

_____

_____

8) It is BEST FOR ME to invite people to church as…

_____

_____

9) It is BEST FOR ME to pray for missionaries and others at…

_____

_____

10) It is BEST FOR ME to give to God's work when…

_____

_____

Take time to talk about some of their answers. Do not embarrass any student for his/her answer, but if you feel led, talk privately with some who have misconceived ideas.

Projected Results:

The students will open up and reveal their inner thoughts and discuss doing their best for Jesus as they realize it is BEST FOR THEM.

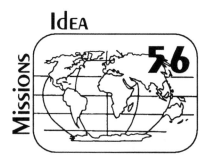

Barrel Packs

Purpose:

> To help the students see the varied needs of foreign missionaries and also home missionaries.

Preparation:

> None

Supplies Needed:

> Circle of chairs

Time Needed:

> 6-10 minutes

What to do:

> Explain to the students, "We are going to play "BARREL PACKS," a game of remembering from the beginning to the end! I will say, 'As I was collecting items for my missionary BARREL PACKS, I put in an **A**larm clock' " (or any item that a missionary could use beginning with an "A").
>
> Each time an item is added to the "BARREL PACKS," it must begin with the next letter of the alphabet, plus it must be something a missionary would need as he/she serves the Lord. The next person to the left adds something beginning with a "B," but they must also say the previous item as well.
>
> "As I was collecting items for my missionary BARREL PACKS, I put in an **A**larm clock and a **B**lanket" (or any item that a missionary would use, as long as it begins with a "B").

The third person would say: "As I was collecting items for my missionary BARREL PACKS, I put in an **A**larm clock, a **B**lanket, and a **C**ookie sheet." And so on. The game continues until the students reach "Z." Advise the students that missionaries need practical things as well as special books and Bibles. (Think up your own penalty if a person cannot add an item.)

Conclude the time with a prayer for the needs of the missionaries, plus ask God to show the class what they might do to help some missionary.

Projected Results:

An opportunity to think about all that a missionary needs in order to serve the Lord, and perhaps stimulate a desire to help a missionary in a practical way.

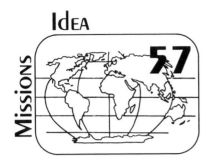

Idea

Missions

57

Add-A-Letter

Purpose:

To let the students have a break from serious study and to concentrate on service words

Preparation:

None

Supplies Needed:

Chairs in a circle

Time Needed:

5-8 minutes

What to do:

Explain to the students: We are going to play a game called: ADD-A-LETTER. I'll begin by saying, "I'm thinking of a word that will help me serve the Lord. It begins with P." (The teacher must have a word in mind. This time it is "PRAYER.")

The student to the teacher's left adds a letter and has an opportunity to guess. If that student doesn't add the right letter, or doesn't guess the word, the next student adds another letter and may guess the word. The game keeps going around the circle, with each student adding a letter until the word is guessed. The one who guesses, gets to start the next game by saying:

"I'm thinking of a word that will help me serve the Lord. It begins with T." (That student must have a word in mind. The word might be "TEACH.")

If a student picks a word that seems unrelated to serving the Lord, ask for an explanation and if he/she can relate it, it counts; if not, the child to his/her left can start the next word. You can also make this a memory game by having the student relate all of the words and the names of the people who said them before giving his/hers. You could also have each player think of a word which begins with the next letter of the alphabet.

Projected Results:

The students will be better able to listen to the rest of the lesson time. They will also have had some important words implanted in their minds.

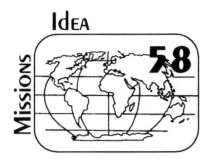

IdEA

58

Missions

World Puzzle

Purpose:

To bring the world before the students' minds and hearts so they can see it as a vast place needing the gospel and as individual lands with individual people and needs.

Preparation:

Find a list of the church missionaries and the countries in which they serve. Make two outline maps by tracing or copying a large world map. Go over the countries' borders on both maps with a thick felt-tipped marker to make them more obvious. On one of the maps, cut out the countries where your church missionaries are located. Place the countries in a pile on the table. On the other map, print in large letters at the top:

"ALL THE ENDS OF THE WORLD SHALL
REMEMBER AND TURN UNTO THE LORD."
(Psalm 22:27a)

Place the whole map on an easel with a solid backing like heavy cardboard or chalkboard.

Supplies Needed:

Large world map, two large papers, same size as map, thick felt-tip black marker, glue or cellophane tape, easel, cardboard or chalkboard for map backing

Time Needed:

6-7 minutes

What to do:

Place the cut-out map pieces of individual nations in a pile in the center of the table, ready to be used. Place the other outline map on the easel. Begin by taking a country outline and, by using some glue or cellophane tape, place the country where it ought to be in the world. As the country is glued in place, the teacher, and then each student, should call out the name of the missionary, the country and then the Bible verse on the map. Go around the class. Each student adds a country until all the countries are placed in their correct positions on the map.

Projected Results:

The students will enjoy the map work; they will see where their missionaries are serving; they will memorize a Bible verse on missions without even trying! And, they will gain valuable help in geography which should benefit them in school.

Alternative:

Do a cut-out map of your country and its states and provinces (or your state/province with its counties/boroughs). If your church does not have missionaries within the state or country, have students think of a mission-type need that the people in that location would have, write that on the outline and then glue or tape it to the outlined map. This will help them think of ways to be witnesses and servants "at home." Each student should call out the name of the missionary or the need in that area (a group or industry that needs the Lord), and then the Bible verse on the map. Go around the class. Each student adds another need until all the states/provinces/counties/boroughs are placed in their correct positions on the map.

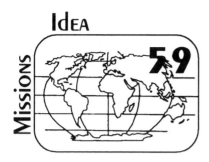

Idea 59

Missions

Bible=Yes/Bible=No

Purpose:

To help the students to see attitudes that agree with the Bible and attitudes that do not agree with the Bible.

Preparation:

Print the DECISION STATEMENTS on cards

Supplies Needed:

Cards, pen, playing surface

Time Needed:

Approximately 12–13 minutes

What to do:

Place the individual cards, upside-down, on the table. Explain that each student will have a turn, starting to the left of the teacher. If there is time, keep playing until all the cards are used. Each student takes the top card and reads it aloud. Then they declare: BIBLE=YES or BIBLE=NO. It depends whether it is an attitude that agrees with the Bible or not. The class then votes to see whether the student is right or wrong. The teacher is the final judge, even over the class vote.

DECISION STATEMENTS to print on cards:
1) I must obey my parents only if they are present.
2) I should tell the truth always.
3) I can cheat on a test if I really don't have time to study.
4) I can avoid other kids if I don't like their religion.
5) I should be kind to everyone.

6) I don't have to read my Bible on busy days.
7) I shouldn't be concerned for people in other lands.
8) I don't have to talk about Jesus if I live a good life for Him.
9) I should always try to get more things.
10) I ought to consider being a missionary.
11) I can give to missions when I'm older, not now.
12) I can do what I want until I graduate from high school.
13) I can talk about people if they are really bad and it's the truth.
14) I should pray for people who need Jesus.
15) I should never do anything with people who don't love Jesus.
16) I can date anyone I want as long as I marry a Christian.
17) I can try smoking as long as I don't get hooked.
18) I ought to try some sins so I can help others overcome them.
19) I should memorize verses from the Bible so I can share them with others.
20) I can take something that doesn't belong to me as long as no one sees me.
21) I can say swear words if I am very angry.
22) I don't have to go to church if I am too busy.
23) I can pray at church, but it isn't necessary at home.
24) I can look for lonely people and make friends with them.
25) I can tell God I am willing to serve Him.
26) I can keep extra change a store clerk gives me by mistake.
27) I can gossip about someone as long as what I say is true.
28) I can damage someone's property and not make it right as long as it was just an accident.
29) I can think anything I want as long as I don't say hurtful things.
30) I can pray silently any time, anywhere, with anyone.

Projected Results:

The students will realize the importance of every decision, thought, or daily action being submitted to God for His approval. We cannot set our own rules or standards for living! They will begin to evaluate their actions by the standard of: Is this what Jesus wants me to do?

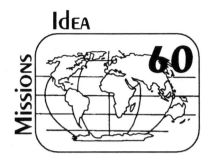

IdEA

Missions

60

WHO CARES?

PURPOSE:

To give a challenge to the class and to show them that God wants them to share.

PREPARATION:

Five copies of the script

Supplies Needed:

Copier and paper, stage area

Time Needed:

6-7 minutes

What to do:

Divide the class into five groups: QUESTIONERS, DOUBTERS, SKEPTICS, SCRIPTORS, and BELIEVERS. Give them the script and have them speak loudly, in unison. If they do well, try it in front of other classes. If it goes well there, try it in front of the entire church.

QUESTIONERS: I'm lonely, oh so lonely.
DOUBTERS: Who cares?
SKEPTICS: That's life. Go see a psychiatrist.
SCRIPTORS: Jesus said, "I WILL NEVER LEAVE THEE, NOR FORSAKE THEE" (Hebrews 13:5A).
BELIEVERS: Praise God, He's always there.

QUESTIONERS: I feel so awful. I've sinned. I've done so many bad things.
DOUBTERS: Who cares?
SKEPTICS: Don't worry, just go have fun and don't

think about it.

SCRIPTORS: "FOR THE WAGES OF SIN IS DEATH; BUT THE GIFT OF GOD IS ETERNAL LIFE THROUGH JESUS CHRIST OUR LORD" (Romans 6:23).

BELIEVERS: God forgives our sins when we trust Jesus as our Saviour.

QUESTIONERS: Won't any religion get us to Heaven?

DOUBTERS: Who cares?

SKEPTICS: Of course, the Hindu, the idol worshippers, the Moslems. They all know God in their own way.

SCRIPTORS: "JESUS SAITH TO HIM, I AM THE WAY, THE TRUTH, AND THE LIFE: NO MAN COMETH UNTO THE FATHER, BUT BY ME" (John 14:6).

BELIEVERS: Jesus said He was the only way to Heaven and we believe Him.

QUESTIONERS: Then you believe the heathen are lost?

DOUBTERS: That's ridiculous. Such a narrow-minded attitude!

SKEPTICS: Of course God wouldn't condemn those who haven't heard.

SCRIPTORS: "FOR THE GRACE OF GOD THAT BRINGETH SALVATION HATH APPEARED TO ALL MEN" (Titus 2:11).

BELIEVERS: There is only one way of salvation. We must believe God's Word and trust Jesus alone for salvation.

QUESTIONERS: If that is true, why aren't all the Christians out witnessing and supporting missionaries around the world?

DOUBTERS: Who cares?

SKEPTICS: The grave is the end of everything.

SCRIPTORS: "...GO OUT INTO THE HIGHWAYS AND HEDGES, AND COMPEL THEM TO COME IN, THAT MY HOUSE MAY BE FILLED" (Luke 14:23).

BELIEVERS: Lord, make us missionaries, at home or overseas.

Projected Results:

Joy in proclaiming the missionary message as the students answer some of their own questions.